D0119454

THE
DAD'S
POCKET BIBLE

THE
DAD'S
POCKET BIBLE

STEPHEN GILES

PB POCKET BIBLES

This edition first published in Great Britain 2010 by
Crimson Publishing, a division of Crimson Business Ltd
Westminster House
Kew Road
Richmond
Surrey
TW9 2ND

© Stephen Giles, 2010

The right of Stephen Giles to be identified as the author of this work has
been asserted by him in accordance with the Copyright, Designs and
Patents Act, 1988.

All rights reserved. No part of this publication may be reproduced,
transmitted in any form or by any means, or stored in a retrieval system
without either the prior written permission of the publisher, or in the case
of reprographic reproduction a licence issued in accordance with the
terms and licences issued by the CLA Ltd.

A catalogue record for this book is available from the British Library.

ISBN 978 1 907087 028

Printed and bound by Lego Print SpA, Trento

ACKNOWLEDGEMENTS

This book is dedicated to Oliver and George, without whom it would be pointless.

I owe my thanks to the dads I surveyed for the book, including Steve Fountain, Tony Luton and Barry Giles. Thanks also to Beth Bishop at Crimson, Hannah Doran for her parenting wisdom, and, as ever, to Sarah for keeping it all together.

CONTENTS

INTRODUCTION

It doesn't matter who my father was; it matters who I remember he was.
Anne Sexton

Being a dad these days can be a fairly bewildering business. Gone are the days when the father's only input into family life was to administer a few thwacks of the cane before disappearing off to the club to smoke cigars and swirl brandy with his pals.

These days, dads are young, old, middle-aged, single, married, divorced, hands-on, hands-off, rich, poor and all points in between. Whoever you are and whatever your situation, the only thing your children can ask of you is to be the best dad you can in the time you have.

American cartoonist Bill Watterson's superb creation *Calvin and Hobbes* offers a huge range of insights into family life – one of the most memorable is when the father of the eternal six-year-old hero Calvin reflects on his own life, deciding that he wouldn't have been in such a rush to grow up if he'd known that so much of adulthood was ad libbed. It's a feeling that a lot of us can echo – knowing that our children will turn to us throughout our lives looking for certainty when we don't always have a clue ourselves can be pretty worrying.

But now you have a fighting chance of finding the answers to most of the questions that life – and fatherhood – throws at you. *The Dad's Pocket Bible* isn't a parenting book, it's a survival manual for the combined role of social worker, taxi driver, financial manager, cook, bouncer, coach, referee, nurse and children's entertainer that modern fatherhood has become. From car problems to emotional crises, from nappies to blocked drains and from midweek dinners to father-of-the-bride speeches, everything in here is created with your every need in mind.

Whatever kind of dad you are or want to be, one important goal is to face the challenges with a smile. You'll find plenty to smile about in these pages: whether it's facts, insights, pocket tips or just simply the answers to those irritating questions that your kids will insist on asking you . . .

THE APPLE OF YOUR EYE: BABIES AND TODDLERS

To be a successful father there's one absolute rule: when you have a kid don't look at it for the first two years.
Ernest Hemingway

🚗 THE NEW DAD 🚗

Congratulations to you if you're a new dad. You'll be elated, and probably just a little bit terrified. Suddenly you've got a life to look after, wash, feed and change. Now, this might come naturally to some, but even the modern dad needs some pointers. Here's your *Dad's Pocket Bible* guide to the essentials of caring for a very small baby.

NEWBORN BABIES: THE SURPRISING FACTS

- Their first poos are dark and sticky. The dark sticky stuff, called meconium, will soon give way to something yellow or green and runny (in breastfed babies) and paler and firmer (and generally smellier) in formula-fed.

- Their skin is very often flaky, blotchy, spotty or it has a rash. (Check with your health visitor if you're worried, but in most cases it will be harmless and normal.)

- They may be very hairy. This is the remains of lanugo, the covering that protected them in the womb, and will drop out soon.

- They may also still have vernix on them, and so be a bit greasy. Don't bother trying to wash it off, as it'll help protect against dry skin.

- Their head might be a weird shape, squished by the journey down the birth canal (especially if vacuum extraction or forceps were used to ease them out). The soft spot on the top, where the skull bones have yet to fuse, is called the fontanelle. It's likely to be a year or more before it closes up.

- Their eyes may squint. This is because the muscles round them have yet to develop.

- The remains of the umbilical cord stays attached to their belly for a few weeks after birth, after which it shrivels and drops off. Let your midwife or health visitor know if it looks sore, as it can sometimes become infected.

- They may sleep for hours and hours on end during the day in the first few weeks (but probably not all at the same time!) Make the most of this time to catch up on some rest yourself!

- A baby is born with 300 separate bones. Some of these bones will fuse together later, as adults only have 206 bones.

- A baby can breathe and swallow at the same time until seven months, which an adult cannot.

- Babies are born without kneecaps.

How to . . . change a nappy

Changing a nappy is a simple process as long as you follow the basic rule of being prepared. Preparation is all, and unless you've gone down the washable nappy route it is in the form of a plentiful supply of baby wipes, nappies and nappy sacks.

1. Assemble all necessary kit and a roll of kitchen towels.

2. Get the baby laid down on a safe mat – ideally on the floor. Even at ground level, you're not going to be able to leave the baby alone for long, so it is crucial to have everything to hand before you start.

3. Next, take a couple of sheets of kitchen roll and place them on the mat under the baby's 'business end'. This will help to keep everything dry and will absorb any other potential

leakage. Boys in particular have a habit of weeing everywhere once the nappy is off.

4. Only at this stage should you remove the nappy. Dispose of it immediately: don't leave it lying around where junior can kick it over. Wipe around the bottom and genitals – with a girl wipe away from the vagina to avoid infection; with a boy clean all around the foreskin on the penis but don't pull it back. Once you've given the whole area a good wipe – even if it's just a pee nappy – use another sheet of kitchen roll to very gently pat the area dry.

5. Now get the new nappy on. Disposable nappies use fastening tape, which is invariably secured at the front, across the baby's abdomen. Make sure it's not too tight: you should be able to get your thumb between nappy and skin.

6. Finally, seal the discarded nappy with the elastic tabs, put it in a nappy bag and then in the bin. Wash your hands and you're done.

Pocket tip 🍺

To deal with nappy rash, leave your baby's nappy off as long as you can – lay them on a towel to catch any mess. Use a barrier cream or petroleum jelly to protect the affected area and avoid using baby wipes – just plain water and cotton wool will do the trick. If the rash persists for more than a couple of days, speak to your health visitor or GP about stronger treatments.

KEY DEVELOPMENTAL STAGES

Most healthy babies will reach the same developmental milestones as their peers at roughly the same time. If you are concerned that your baby is not on track, contact your health visitor or GP for an assessment.

• By three months, a baby should be able to smile, gurgle and focus.

- By six months, a baby should be able to roll over, reach and grab things.

- By nine months, a baby should be able to sit unaided, laugh and enjoy simple 'peekaboo' games.

- By 12 months, a baby should be able to pull themselves into a standing position.

- By 18 months, a baby should be able to walk and form basic recognisable words.

- By two years, a baby should be able to connect words, feed themselves and kick a ball.

- By three years, a toddler should be able to form complete sentences, may well be toilet trained and able to perform complex motor skills – such as jumping, hopping and climbing – independently.

Pocket fact 🔔

Every day approximately 395,000 babies are born and approximately 145,000 people die. If the world's population continues to grow at the current rate it will be 15 billion by the end of this century.

WHAT SHOULD THEY WEAR?

There are two specific functions of baby clothes. Firstly, there are the clothes that you dress the baby in to have pictures taken, go for walks and visit friends and relatives. These clothes are often unbelievably cute designer wear modelled on a micro version of your own fashions. Invariably they are expensive, fairly uncomfortable and a bit fiddly when nappy change time comes around.

The amount of time, money and effort you put into sourcing these clothes depends entirely on the amount of vicarious pleasure you will get from seeing your baby dressed in Gucci jeans.

Then there is the second category – clothes for living. These are the clothes that your baby will have on 95% of the time: for playing, eating and sleeping. Romper suits are the best bet – preferably not in white – though long-sleeved T-shirts and trousers with integral feet are also great for the first six months.

Pocket tip 🍺

Although you should keep clothing simple, try to avoid the cheapest options on the market – very low grade clothes won't wash well and may lose their shape really quickly.

WHAT BABY KIT IS REALLY NECESSARY?

At birth a baby needs somewhere to sleep, some clothes, nappies, and a car seat if you're planning to travel anywhere. In theory, nothing else is 'essential' kit. Most people, however, want their child to have far more than just the basics. The following are on most standard lists of 'must-have' baby kit.

Pushchair

Or more likely, two pushchairs. One of these needs to be a good, solid all-terrain vehicle that can be pushed around fields, country lanes and even along the uneven pavements of most cities. The other needs to be small, lightweight and sufficiently compact that it can be folded and carried by either parent. This second type is ideal for bus and train journeys or for quick trips around town.

When choosing a pushchair, consider practicalities before looks:

● Will it fit into the boot of your car?

● Does it have pneumatic tyres? These are prone to frequent punctures and are a real pain to replace.

● Is the folding mechanism simple to use, or will it break easily?

● Does the pushchair have storage space for nappy bags and other kit?

- If you're buying from the higher end of the market, what is the lifespan of the pushchair? It's much better to buy a pushchair that transforms from a pram to a baby buggy to a toddler's chair.

- Does the pushchair have a decent, low centre of gravity? Fashionable high-level pushchairs may be good for parent-baby interaction but they're not so hot when they topple over, courtesy of the heavy shopping bag on the handle.

Pocket tip 🍺

If you've got friends with a pushchair, take it out for a quick road test before you commit to your own purchase.

Backpack/sling/baby carrier

These have been lumped together, but in truth they have roles in very different stages of baby development. The sling is useful in the first couple of months, when the baby isn't really moving around, whereas the baby carrier is best when there's a greater degree of neck control and the baby can enjoy a view of the word around.

The backpack is possibly the most versatile bit of kit, as it can be used from about six months until the baby becomes too heavy to lug around. Most models are lightweight and easy to take on and off – though it's worth checking you can do this unaided. Again, a simple road test in the shop will help you find the best and most comfortable option. You can get backpacks from kids' shops like Mothercare, but they are also sold in camping and out-door shops.

Travel cot

This is a must if you're thinking about going away anywhere. Light and easy to store and transport, they also make great playpens/ball pools down the line.

Swing

A personal favourite, these are a little bit like portable respite care – nothing beats a swing when you just want to dump the baby somewhere safe and entertaining while you get a cup of tea. Some babies love them and will happily snooze away to the bizarre plink-plonk rhythms, while others scream blue murder as soon as they're sat in. Try before you buy.

Operating baby equipment

One word: instructions. It might sound simple, but then that's because it is. Most baby kit is intuitive, from the folding mechanism of a pushchair to fitting a car seat, but if it goes wrong you're facing a complete nightmare, so always check with the store you bought the item from or read the manufacturer's instructions carefully.

This advice is especially important when you're dealing with critical kit like bottle sterilisers and car seats – for more information on this see page 145.

🚗 HOLDING AND FEEDING A BABY 🚗

Holding and feeding your baby for the first time can be pretty nerve-wracking. Follow these simple steps to get you through:

1. Sit down for the first time until you get confident and relaxed.

2. If you are right-handed, bend your left arm to a 90 degree angle. This arm is going to be the base for the baby. The crook of your elbow is the pillow: the forearm should run along their body with your hand supporting the lower half of the baby.

3. Try to relax your arm as much as possible, no matter how tense you may be feeling – you wouldn't like to lie on a rock hard mattress, would you?

4. If you are feeding the baby, take the bottle of milk in your right hand and splash a little on your left wrist to check the temperature. Heat bottles under warm running water; never in the microwave.

5. Tip the bottle sufficiently to fill the whole teat with milk; otherwise the baby will be guzzling air.

6. If the baby stops feeding and won't take any more milk, sit them up on your lap and gently rub or pat their back, starting low and working upwards. This may be the stage where you get a vomit-laden burp, so it can help to have a towel on your lap. On the plus side, there are few things in life more satisfying than hearing a truly deep resonant belch coming from your offspring. That is, until they do it in a restaurant.

7. Continue the feeding/burping process until the baby is no longer interested.

It's worth the wait

Reassure your partner with the following statistics. Animals with a longer gestation than humans include:

- *Elephant (approx 638 days)*
- *Giraffe (420 days)*
- *Camel (405 days)*
- *Zebra (390 days)*
- *Whale (360 days)*
- *Horse (335 days)*

(The average human pregnancy lasts just 270 days. What a breeze!)

WHEN AND WHAT SHOULD YOUR BABY EAT?

Babies don't really 'eat' until they are six months old. Some start eating puréed food earlier, from about four months. Generally speaking, you'll get a good idea if the baby is ready to start solids if milk feeds no longer seem to be sufficient or if the baby shows interest in food and chewing. Weaning (the process of gradually introducing solids into a baby's diet) is usually the first time a dad can make a significant contribution to feeding, so it's good bonding time.

Signs that your baby is ready for solids:

- They are able to hold their head up straight and can sit upright when supported.

- They are demanding more frequent milk feeds and seem unsatisfied afterwards.

- They are waking with hunger having previously slept through the night.

- Their birth weight has approximately doubled.

Good first weaning foods include baby rice and cereal, then move on to puréed vegetables and fruit mixed with some breast milk or formula. Try one new flavour at a time as babies can be pretty picky. It's also a good way to identify possible food intolerances.

Five tasty purées:

- Butternut squash and pear
- Apple and carrot
- Avocado and banana
- Courgette and potato
- Dried fruit compote

After a few weeks, you can try grown-up cereal (like Weetabix), again mushed up with some warm milk. Most of your baby's food will be a puréed mush until about 12 months, when it starts to be a bit easier to digest solids. In the early days of weaning, be prepared for some strange and stinky nappies.

Pocket tip 🍺

A 'meal' for a baby of six months plus is about three rounded teaspoons of food.

When you're weaning, start with one solid meal a day, see how it goes and ramp up the number of meals over the following month or so until you're giving the baby three meals a day around your own meal times. From 12 months onwards your child's diet should broadly resemble your own – though steer clear of the chicken vindaloo. Chopped up meat, boneless fish or even baby-sized pasta shapes are all fine early foods.

Pocket tip 🍺

From around eight to nine months old, most babies are ready to try snack foods, like slices of apple, cooked carrot sticks, slivers of flat bread like tortilla, or thin slices of cheese. Don't ever give honey to a child under one year of age, or leave a baby to eat alone.

Five first finger foods (from six months):

- Rusks: toast fingers in the oven
- Rice cakes, unsalted
- Hardboiled egg
- Apple slices
- Carrot sticks, steamed

FOOD ALLERGIES

These sometimes come out in weaning babies, especially those who are given cow's milk, eggs or nuts. All three of these should be avoided in the first year of a child's life at least. Ultimately, if your toddler gets sick after eating or drinking a particular type of food you may need to go to a dietician for advice on food allergies. Allergies should not be underestimated: they can cause death in extreme cases.

Pocket fact 🥄

More people are allergic to cow's milk than to any other food in the world.

🚗 BATHING A BABY 🚗

Bath time is a potentially great opportunity for you to have some special moments alone with your baby. Some babies love the experience and some hate it. There's a tendency to make a bath part of the whole bedtime wind-down but there really is no need to give your baby a full bath every day. In fact, some of the soaps and bubble baths around could actually harm your baby's skin if used too frequently. Instead of a daily bath, just give your baby a daily 'top and tail' wash, cleaning the head neck and nappy area with warm water and cotton wool.

Pocket tip 🍺

Never *leave a baby alone in a bath, even if you're just popping out to answer the phone or door.*

How to . . . bath a baby

You can bath the little one every two to three days. Follow these simple steps for a stress-free soak:

1. Make sure you've got everything you'll need close to hand in the bathroom. This includes a towel, new nappy, clean clothes, cloth or cotton wool, and mild soap.

2. Run the bath with cold water first. Use a bath thermometer to get the bathwater temperature up to around 38°C. Mild bubble bath is ok – some are lavender scented for night-time relaxation.

3. The water should be around 10cm deep. If your baby is sitting up, run the bath to waist depth.

4. Put your baby into the bath, or bath seat, supporting the head and neck.

5. Use a soft cloth or flannel to clean your baby, starting with the eyes and face, or gently splash with water. Use bath books or plastic toys to calm and engage your baby.

6. When you've finished, take the baby out of the bath and wrap in a soft towel. Pat them dry and allow the skin to breathe before you put nappy and clothes on. If your baby has nappy rash, put some skin cream on once the skin is dry.

🚗 COMMON CHILDHOOD 🚗
ILLNESSES

Colic

Between one and three hours a day of wailing is quite normal, and very often it's for no discernible reason.

Up to a fifth of babies suffer from 'excessive' crying, which is usually called colic. No-one's really sure why exactly this happens, although there are plenty of theories – the most popular is that it's due to pain caused by an immature digestive system.

- If your baby's crying relentlessly, check they're not hungry, tired, in need of a feed, or poorly.

- If it's none of those things, then work your way through a list of potential solutions: try holding, cuddling, jiggling, rocking, swinging, singing, going for a walk or a drive.

- There are various commercial preparations, such as Infacol, which are said to help with colic – these won't definitely help, but you may feel it's worth a shot.

- Check with your health visitor or GP if you have a problem with a relentlessly crying baby, as once in a while, there'll be a medical reason for their distress.

The good news about colic is that it almost always eases up by the time your baby is about three months old.

High temperature

This may come as a result of a bug (along with vomiting, see page 13), or may be caused by a reaction to the jabs your baby needs at two to four months and 12–13 months. Most high temperatures can be brought down by a dose of baby paracetamol solution. Check with the chemist for suitable treatments and dosage instructions. If the temperature persists, see your doctor.

Meningitis

This one's not a common problem thankfully, but one you need to be aware of, as it can be a very virulent and deadly illness. It comes in two forms: viral and bacterial. Viral meningitis is a mild disease that has similar symptoms to flu. It usually doesn't need medical treatment, though you should make sure your baby doesn't get dehydrated.

Bacterial meningitis can be more severe – as well as flu-like symptoms, it can be diagnosed from severe pain in the hands or legs, if hands and legs are cold, or if the skin is pale and the lips are blue.

Other possible signs of meningitis in babies include:

- Lack of responsiveness
- Irritability
- Vomiting
- Uncontrollable crying
- Blotchy skin
- A stiff body with jerky movements, or can be lifeless and floppy

Pocket tip 🍺

If your baby has meningitis symptoms including blotchy skin, place a clear glass gently against the skin – if the rash doesn't disappear under gentle pressure, call 999.

DEALING WITH SICK

What goes in must come out, and while the expulsion is normally managed in an orderly fashion in the nappy area, sometimes you can be taken by surprise by a bout of projectile vomiting. Milk is especially nasty as it becomes sour and smelly very quickly, so you've no real option but to completely change all the baby's affected clothes and probably wash the poor soul's face and hair too.

Pocket tip 🍺

Some people cannot stand the smell of sick. If you feel this way, block your nose with tissues. Try sucking a peppermint while you clean: the saliva may help you avoid nausea and the aroma will fill your sinuses.

There are two main types of baby vomit. The first is the reflux gag, which happens when wind is trapped on the wrong side of milk, forcing it back up and out. There's not much you can do about that one, except to burp the baby a bit more gently (see above).

There is also an illness known as GORD (Gastro Oesophageal Reflux Disease) which can result in frequent vomiting, so consult your doctor if the milk comes back up regularly. The trick here is to minimise food intake but to keep the baby hydrated. Ease off the milk for a while and substitute water – you can also get a powder from the chemist that will help you re-hydrate a sick baby.

🚗 PATERNITY LEAVE AND 🚗 BONDING WITH YOUR BABY

Spending time with your newborn is a challenge. Although paternity leave regulations are set to change, allowing dads to have up to three months off with their babies, at the moment the statutory leave period remains at two weeks. The money paid by the state to fathers during this period is just over £100 per week which explains why most of us can't afford to spend longer with the family.

But there are practical steps you can take to make your time as meaningful as possible:

1. Don't take it immediately. Your partner may well be inundated with offers of help in the early stages – take advantage of this by staying at work for the immediate aftermath of the birth. Then take your leave a couple of weeks later when things have settled down a bit.

2. Extend it with holiday. With a newborn in tow, you may not be able to jet off for summer sun this year, so why not use that annual leave to boost your paternity leave period? Learning the ropes at this early stage is vital for your confidence as a father, so take the chance to get stuck in.

3. Be an evening or weekend hero. If you are back at work, you can still make a huge contribution to the bonding process by devoting as much of your evening and weekend time to the baby. This will score you points with your exhausted partner, but it will also allow you to gain even more confidence managing baby alone. Long weekend walks and nights spent playing on the living room floor are also pretty good ways to unwind at the end of a stressful day.

4. Don't sweat the home stuff. If you're coming home every day to piles of washing up and dirty nappies it's pretty tempting to throw yourself into the role of domestic god and clean up after mum and baby. But tidying the house won't get you any closer to your little one. Instead, enlist the help of friends and family to help with the chores, or spend a little money hiring a cleaner or laundry service while you get back on your feet.

What I wish I'd known: Top advice from dads

- *There is such a thing as post-natal depression for dads.*
- *Once your kids hit the age of four and can feed themselves, use the toilet themselves and recognise danger, they become one hell of a lot easier to handle.*
- *Never, ever take sides – either with one child against another or with your children against your partner. It will always come back to bite you.*
- *Don't expect too much.*
- *Make sure that you and your partner have quality time together and never take each other for granted.*
- *Save all the money you can – you're going to need it.*

- *Buy toys second hand.*
- *You can never have too many batteries.*
- *Don't ever worry about making a fool of yourself. Just do it.*
- *You cannot demand respect from your kids – you can only earn it.*

Top ten TV dads

- *Homer Simpson* (The Simpsons)
- *Fred Flintstone* (The Flintstones)
- *Al Bundy* (Married with Children)
- *Dr. Heathcliff Huxtable* (The Cosby Show)
- *Charles Ingalls* (Little House on the Prairie)
- *Tony Soprano* (The Sopranos)
- *Jack Bauer* (24)
- *Peter Griffin* (Family Guy)
- *Jim Royle* (The Royle Family)
- *'Dirty' Den Watts* (East Enders)

2

YOUNG CHILDREN: KEEPING THEM HAPPY

One father is worth more than a hundred schoolmasters.
George Herbert

Once you've got past the baby years you suddenly find yourself as the father of a responsive, alert information sponge. Your child is desperate for you to pass on all the pearls of wisdom you've been saving up all these years. But where do you start? You may never forget how to ride a bike, but do you remember how you learned? Don't worry, all the essential skills are explained in the following chapter.

🚗 READING 🚗

Teach your child to . . . improve their reading and writing

Start at the beginning

Good learning practice begins at home and it begins early. Survey after survey tells us that children who have bedtime stories develop a better vocabulary, greater love of reading and become more academically skilled. So why don't we all read stories as a matter of course?

Time is the biggest factor restricting us, but even a five-minute session with an old favourite will engender a real interest, so it really does pay to start early. As you read, point out words and associations – a three-month-old baby will enjoy the sounds and movements of a lively tale just as much as a six-year old.

The (unofficial) top five books for 0–6-year-olds

Any list of books is subjective, but here are some all-time classics that must be at the heart of any library:

1.	The Very Hungry Caterpillar	*Eric Carle*
2.	Where the Wild Things Are	*Maurice Sendak*
3.	Dear Zoo	*Rod Campbell*
4.	The Gruffalo	*Julia Donaldson and Axel Scheffler*
5.	Winnie the Pooh stories	*A.A. Milne*

Pocket fact

The Very Hungry Caterpillar was first published in 1969, and has sold over 30 million copies worldwide. It is widely regarded as one of the best children's books ever written.

Encourage a love of books

Libraries are a fantastic free resource and a great place for all children to discover that books are about more than just learning. Most libraries have dedicated children's sections with comfortable furniture and even toys to play with while they just relax in that environment. Don't worry if your child doesn't always want to read books, and don't be too obsessed with silence – libraries have come a long way since the days of harsh, dusty spinster librarians in half-moon specs glaring at anyone who breathes too loudly. Now many have story time at least once a week, holiday activities and brilliant 'story sacks', which include a book along with all the props you need to make a story come alive.

The (unofficial) top five books for 6–10 year-olds

Again, it's just a selection, but these are more essential, wonderful classics:

1.	Charlotte's Web	*E.B. White*
2.	Swallows and Amazons	*Arthur Ransome*
3.	The Sheep-Pig	*Dick King-Smith*
4.	The Machine Gunners	*Robert Westall*
5.	The Wind in the Willows	*Kenneth Grahame*

Use technology to support tradition

Books are great but they aren't the only way to improve under-standing. You can buy interactive learning systems such as *Leapfrog*, which are adaptable to suit all ages and that specifically help children with spelling by teaching phonics, a method of teaching reading based on sound recognition. These systems are available from toy stores. Additionally, internet resources such as those on the CBeebies website (www.bbc.co.uk/cbeebies) offer great opportunities to support learning with play. For a more detailed list of websites that support learning see page 66.

Pocket tip 🍺

Mnemonics (memorable rhymes or phrases that aid recall) are a great way to help your child learn key facts. One classic example lists the colours of the rainbow in sequence: red, orange, yellow, green, blue, indigo and violet; using an example from history: 'Richard Of York Gave Battle In Vain'. Two key facts in one — what a bargain!

Give your time

The greatest thing you can do is to give your time to your child's learning. Reading to your child is step one, and that carries on for years, but actually just reading near your child is another way of helping them feel that reading is a pleasure. Talk about words and sounds, do puzzles and play games with your child, make up silly rhymes and stories that allow them to spot patterns of language.

Pocket tip 🍺

Gently correct your child's grammar by repeating an incorrect statement back to them as a checking question. You don't have to point out the mistake, just keep giving them positive input. For example: 'I sawed a bird' becomes, 'You saw a bird?'

How to . . . read a bedtime story

It's not always easy to summon up the energy to read a bedtime story at the end of the day, but it's a wonderful way to foster a love of books, as well as a great way to catch up. By personalising the stories you can make this an incredibly special bonding time with your child.

1. **How long should the story be?** It depends on your child's age and attention span, but 20 minutes is about right for most. Older children will enjoy a serial story, with a cliff-hanger ending each night. Younger children like complete stories, and they also like the same formula again and again, so don't be surprised if you need to keep repeating favourite stories or plotlines.

2. **What story should you choose?** As mentioned above, you may not always get the choice if certain stories become firm favourites. But to keep the choice wide – and to preserve your sanity – you could try to build in a regular trip to the library for new and different books to read. You'll find lists of popular classics in this chapter.

3. **Do it yourself.** While storybooks have a great visual appeal, there's nothing quite as good as a story made up off the cuff. It might sound daunting to invent new tales every night, but you can turn story time into a really dynamic and interactive time by getting your child to name the characters, decide on locations, weather and other details. Make your descriptions really vivid so that your child can picture all the sights, sounds and tastes of your story in their head. Bring in real-life characters – members of the family, friends and teachers. And make sure it all ends happily ever after.

Top ten bedtime stories: picture books

1. *Say Goodnight*	*Helen Oxenbury*
2. *Hippos Go Beserk*	*Sandra Boynton*
3. *The Runaway Dinner*	*Allan Ahlberg and Bruce Ingman*
4. *We're Going on a Bear Hunt*	*Michael Rosen and Helen Oxenbury*

5. *Maisy's Bedtime*	*Lucy Cousins*
6. *I am not Sleepy and I Will Not go to Bed*	*Lauren Child*
7. *Moonlight*	*Jan Ormerod*
8. *My First Oxford Book of Poems*	*John Foster*
9. *The Twelve Dancing Princesses*	*The Brothers Grimm and Jane Ray*
10. *Each Peach Pear Plum*	*Janet and Allan Ahlberg*

🚗 SPORTS 🚗

Teach your child to . . . ride a bike

A steady start

Confidence is the key when your child starts cycling.

- Adjust the seat of the bike so that your child is able to comfortably reach the ground with their toes on either side while seated on the saddle. If they can't do this, the bike is too big.

- Give your child a helmet and elbow/knee protectors, even if the chances of falling off the bike at this stage are reduced. It's a lot easier than trying to introduce the safety aspect at a later stage.

- Fit stabilisers to the bike so that your child can master the key concepts of steering and pedalling. If these are done separately from the main event of balancing, they will already be engrained when the stabilisers come off.

Pocket tip 🍺

When your child steers a bike for the first time, it is natural for them to focus on obstacles, such as trees and fences. Unfortunately, this focus will translate into movements towards that object and will often involve a nasty collision. Encourage your child to concentrate always on the way ahead, being aware of obstacles, but not focused on them.

Removing the stabilisers

When you have removed the stabilisers from the bike, you will need to try out your child's sense of balance for the first time.

- Go somewhere with a gentle slope, lots of space and some-thing soft (like grass) to fall onto, as your child will, inevitably, fall off – probably several times.

- Make sure your child is well protected against falls with sensi-ble clothing.

- Guide your child with a hand on the back of the saddle and then let go, allowing your child to ride freely, but keeping pace with them so as to be ready to catch hold again in case of a wobble.

- You need to repeat the above process plenty of times, and give lots of praise and encouragement for all the times your child rides unaided.

- If your child falls over, don't make a big deal of it. Pick them up and encourage them to give it another go soon after.

- Once you're comfortable with their abilities, go a short distance away and get them to ride towards you. Keep increasing that dis-tance until they are covering a lot of ground without you.

The rules of the road

Once your child is confident and comfortable on the bike you'll need to talk about the rules of the road. It's a responsible subject, but you can make it fun. Give them a certificate and a cyclist's highway code and talk about some key road signs, but keep the focus on their safety. Take them out for a bike ride on a quiet day and point out hazards and good practice.

> ### *Bikeability*
>
> *Bikeability is a cycle training programme run by Cycling England and based on the National Standard for Cycle Training, a standard set by the Department of Transport in*

England and Wales. The scheme is for all ages, and replaces the Cycling Proficiency Test which was aimed at children.

There are three levels in the programme:

Level 1 (Red) tests basic skills in a traffic free environment.

Level 2 (Amber) tests essential manoeuvres and common sense on quiet roads.

Level 3 (Green) requires a mastery of complex skills in all traffic conditions.

Teach your child to . . . swim

Confidence in water is more than simply a hobby; it's a potential life-saver, so this is one skill you can't afford to sidestep. Here's some good advice on what to do (and what not to do).

Show through play

Get into the water yourself and demonstrate exactly how much fun it is by playing with a ball, swimming underwater, splashing around or whatever your level of confidence in water allows. The more your child sees you relaxed and having fun, the more they will focus on learning the skills to let them in on it.

Reward interest

If your child does start to take an interest in the water, think about getting hold of accessories like goggles or snorkel sets to help them get used to the idea of putting their heads (and most of all, their eyes) in the water. Further down the line, wetsuits and body-boards are good incentives to take their interest out to the seaside as an all-weather hobby. You might even think about getting a swimming teacher involved if your confidence isn't strong. Make sure you use a variety of teaching aids: you don't want your child to become dependent on one.

Get water confident

Start early: the sooner your child is confident splashing and jumping about, the sooner they will learn essential skills like buoyancy and resistance. Getting your child to dip their head in the water is one of the first steps towards building their confidence. So use plastic toys, balls and other distractions that will get them splashing about and getting their heads wet without distressing them. Bob up and down in the water and get your child to copy you. Then take a deep breath and dip your face underwater, encouraging your child to do the same. Hold your breath and let it out underwater, creating masses of bubbles, and get your child to repeat this.

Strokes of genius

After you've mastered the basics of breathing in the pool, get your child used to floating and relaxing by practising floating on your backs in the shallow end. Your child's first instinct will be to stiffen and panic in the water, but if you support their weight while they lie back and give them plenty of reassurance, eventually they'll relax sufficiently to float in the water. Gently remove your hands from their supporting position, but be ready to help again if your child gets into difficulty.

Don't be dangerous or gung-ho

Everyone knows someone whose dad taught them to swim by chucking them off a cross-channel ferry (or at least into the deep end of the local pool). But for every person who thrives as a result of the 'kill or cure' approach, there are a dozen who are scarred for life by an intensely frightening experience.

Pocket fact
Feodor Vassilyev (1707–1782), a Russian peasant, holds the record for the most kids. He fathered 69 children with his two wives.

Teach your child to . . . play football

The great thing about football is that it is about the easiest game in the world to organise. The old 'jumpers for goalposts' cliché tells us everything we need to know about the basic requirements of a game – that and a ball of course.

Unless you've got your FA coaching badges, you're probably only going to be able to give your child basic support on their journey to Premier League stardom. But if you want to be there every kick of the way the following will help.

Start smaller

The fundamental skills that kids need are about ball control – mainly dribbling, passing and shooting. These can be learned from a young age using an appropriately sized and weighted ball. Work your way up to a full sized ball as your child improves their co-ordination. A young child just needs to have fun and build confidence with a soft ball and a practice goal.

Training matters

As your child gets older and more serious, introduce a relaxed 'training' session. Get some cones in your garden or the local park and make your child dribble the ball around them in a 'slalom'. Set up a shooting 'target' over a child's football goal and encourage your child to practise a range of shooting styles – most children instinctively 'toe-poke' the ball at a young age. Show your child how hitting the ball with the inside and outside of the foot produces different results.

The offside rule

If a player is in their opponents' half when a ball is played to them and that player is closer to the opponents' goal line than the second-to-last player on the opposite side then they are judged to be offside – as long as they are in play and gain an active advantage from receiving the ball. Next question . . .

Steer clear of tricks

Tricks and 'keepie-uppies' are great ways to improve balance, focus and control, but they are not exactly at the heart of the game. Use these to end a training session rather than as a major part.

Follow the game

Watch some football matches on TV with your child – talk them through some of the moves and skills that the best players use. Kids need to know that football is a physical game that needs strength, practice and patience.

Know when to step back

If your child is really interested in the game and wants to get involved with a team, step away from the training and offer your support in other ways, like cheering from the touchline. The team's coaches will thank you for it. This doesn't mean you can't still have a kick-around with your child: in fact, it'll probably be an even more welcome light relief. There are junior leagues in most areas of the country, normally subdivided by age range – under fives, under sevens, under nines and under elevens. The format of the game is similar to the adult version, and sometimes the tackling is even stronger! Teams are usually organised through community centres or schools.

Turn to page 95 for info on how to support from the sidelines.

Football World Cup winners/host nations

1930 – winners Uruguay; hosts Uruguay

1934 – winners Italy; hosts Italy

1938 – winners Italy; hosts France

1950 – winners Uruguay; hosts Brazil

1954 – winners West Germany; hosts Switzerland

1958 – winners Brazil; hosts Sweden

1962 – winners Brazil; hosts Chile

1966 – winners England; hosts England

1970 – winners Brazil; hosts Mexico

1974 – winners West Germany; hosts West Germany

1978 – winners Argentina; hosts Argentina

1982 – winners Italy; hosts Spain

1986 – winners Argentina; hosts Mexico

1990 – winners West Germany; hosts Italy

1994 – winners Brazil; hosts USA
1998 – winners France; hosts France

2002 – winners Brazil; hosts Japan/South Korea
2006 – winners Italy; hosts Germany
2010 – hosts South Africa

Pocket fact

The tournament hosts have won the World Cup six times and Brazil are the current World Cup masters with five victories.

Italy's victory over France in the 2006 World Cup final was watched by an estimated three billion people: half the world's population.

Teach your child to . . . fly a kite

Kites are a lot of fun – they're cheap and pretty easy to use but they aren't always an ideal child's plaything. Supervised practice is essential, especially with a younger child.

1. Buy a cheap starter kite, not the absolute cheapest available but something under a fiver. Match the size and style of kite to the child – if you buy a big, heavy stunt kite you'll end up flying it while your five-year-old stands on the sidelines getting bored.

2. Beaches are ideal places to learn kite skills. Wrap up warm, go in the winter on a Sunday when the beach is empty and let your child get comfortable controlling the basic kite.

3. Get your child to hold the kite above their head in one hand and the string in the other. As soon as the kite starts to take off, get them to let go of it and wind out as much string as possible. If the wind is light, you may need to run with the kite to get it airborne.

4. The more wind there is, the more the kite will dip and soar – fixing a tail to the kite will give it some drag so that it becomes easier to handle in high winds.

Pocket tip 🍺

Never fly the kite near power lines, not even if you feel confident you can control it — the wind is powerful and a child won't necessarily have the same control or strength as you.

Teach your child to . . . tie shoelaces

The most popular way to teach children to tie shoelaces is known as the 'bunny ears' approach. You might need to practise this yourself before you attempt to demonstrate, as it's likely you tie your own laces quickly and it will look complicated. Many children's shoes are now slip on, or use Velcro — but this is still an essential skill to learn! The 'bunny ears' approach works like this:

1. Tie a simple knot with the shoelaces and tighten.

2. Get your child to make the laces into two 'bunny ears'.

3. Demonstrate tying the laces by putting one bunny ear up and the other down and wrapped around.

4. Repeat again and again until the movements become automatic.

5. Get your child to practise as often as possible — and never miss an opportunity to demonstrate how you do it.

🚗 MUSIC 🚗

Teach your child to . . . play a musical instrument

A love of music can become a lifelong passion. If your child shows an interest in playing an instrument, this doesn't necessarily mean you'll be lumbered with endless rehearsal runs or the expense of shelling out for a bunch of underused stringed instruments. Here's how to manage a mini musical maestro.

Choose the instrument with care

Kids have whims and fads and it would be pretty costly if every one of these meant an investment of several hundred pounds in a decent instrument. But it's also important to nurture the interest. Once your child has found an instrument that interests them, develop the interest by hiring an instrument, or by borrowing one. Even getting hold of some CDs featuring the instrument can help to develop your child's ear for what can be done with time and practice.

Buy smart

Once you've decided to take the plunge and buy an instrument, don't forget to check out on-line auctions or even car boot sales for great cheap deals, especially for cumbersome instruments like cellos, drum kits and keyboards. It's an excellent idea to buy second hand – until your child gets *very* good, they will be fine learning on a good quality second hand instrument. Don't be tempted to buy the shiniest in the shop!

Encourage practice

Two mistakes that parents often make are to turn music practice into a chore (or even a punishment in some cases) and to lose enthusiasm. Learning any new skill is a hard slog and most of us don't realise this, especially if we left formal learning behind at school. What is needed is lots of positive reinforcement, and that means sitting through an impromptu concert of your child murdering 'London's Burning' on the recorder for an hour and still heaping praise upon them. Encourage them to practise when you've got some time to spare so you can listen in and support the good work. The more you say, 'Do your violin practice, then you can play', the more it will seem like an obligation to be resented. **It is a hobby, not homework**. They do need to practise to see positive results, but try to help them focus on the progress they're making instead of the length of the journey.

Positive reinforcement

If your child shows commitment to the instrument, reward that with trips to concerts or incentives like a newer, better instrument or membership of a youth orchestra.

Teach your child . . . to whistle

The whistle is a great technique for attracting attention, looking cool and generally irritating people who can't whistle. Here's how you do it:

1. Purse your lips into an 'o' shape, halfway into a kiss.

2. Curl your tongue slightly and keep it low in your mouth, behind your lower teeth.

3. Push air along your tongue and through your pursed lips.

4. Move your tongue to vary the pitch of your whistle.

5. Practise.

🚗 PETS 🚗

Teach your child to . . . care for a pet

Buying a pet can be like having a child – except pets never grow up, never stop needing you and never stop costing you money. But on the upside, they'll always love you no matter what you do. If you've still got very young children, you may want to question the logic of having another dependant mouth to feed and clean up after. Regardless of the pros and cons, children can learn as much from owning a pet as they can from learning a new skill. But it also needs to be given the same careful consideration.

Get some advice

Speak to the RSPCA or a vet about the type of pet you should get your child. Larger pet shops are also good places for advice for prospective owners. Consider the space you have available, the amount of time the pet requires in terms of care, and the cost of equipment – cages, vets fees etc.

Low maintenance is a good start

Even if you desperately want your child to have a Lassie-like companion, you may be as well to start a bit smaller. Children can be full of enthusiasm for a pet in the first flush of novelty, but a dog will live for around 10–15 years depending on the breed. When the novelty wears off you may well be the one who is walking, feeding and caring for your child's pet. So test their pet-owning credentials with a hamster, gerbil, rabbit or guinea pig. Small rodents are ideal starter pets not just because they are relatively easy to care for but also because they have modular cage habitats that can grow as your child's interest grows.

Other good 'starter' pets

These may not be the most interactive critters on the block, but they do at least create interest and a sense of responsibility. They're also very easy to replace if the experiment goes wrong:

- Stick insects
- Goldfish
- Ant farms
- Sea-monkeys

Teach responsibility

Where possible (and without any unnecessary cruelty to the pet), you should give your child responsibility for the animal's welfare. That means they should be taught to handle the pet safely, give food and water, change bedding and play with the pet. Again, anything that feels too much like a chore will only breed resentment of the animal, so make sure your child plays an active part in the whole process: from selecting the pet to caring for it.

You can also make a big difference to the way your child views the pet – never treat the animal badly yourself as your child will imitate your behaviour. Make sure your child respects the animal's need for quiet time and doesn't pester it to play all the time. Encourage good handling practice, showing your child the right way to approach and stroke a dog or to hold another animal.

Pocket fact 🚩

43% of the UK population own a pet.

Reward responsibility

When you do feel that your child is ready to move up to a more time-intensive pet like a cat or dog, go to an animal sanctuary and offer to take some dogs out for walks – they often want volunteers to exercise the 'residents'. It's a great way to get familiar with breeds before making a commitment.

Pocket fact 🏌

The UK's second most popular pets behind cats (approximately nine million) are reptiles. There are more than eight million in UK households, compared with just six and a half million dogs.

Good pet hygiene

Make sure your child follows the basic rules of hygiene if they are to care for the pet. They must always wash their hands after touching the animal or handling bedding and food. All pets should be kept out of bedrooms and must never be fed from plates or allowed to get onto the table. Cages and bedding should be cleaned weekly, and pet hair should be vacuumed regularly. Encourage pets to go outside regularly and keep the house well-ventilated.

Top ten kids' questions and answers

1. **Why is the sky blue?**

   When the rays of the sun strike the atmosphere they clash with particles of dust and other debris that scatter the rays around us. Rays from the red end of the spectrum are not spread so widely, but at the blue end, the rays are dispersed so widely that everything above us looks blue. Turn off the sun and the sky is black. And very cold.

2. **Where did I come from?**

   Good question. The answer will probably depend on the age of your questioner — it doesn't pay to give your child more information than they can handle. A picture book of the body might be a good visual aid. You could start with the simple facts of, 'Daddy plants a seed inside Mummy that grows into a baby', but you're unlikely to get away with that. When you do get down to the mechanics of sex, don't use euphemisms for body parts.

3. *How is a rainbow made?*

You can only see a rainbow when the light of the sun is behind you and it is low in the sky. The rainbow is actually the sun's rays being bent as they enter raindrops, and then reflected at the back of the raindrop before being bent as they emerge again. Different colours are bent at different angles, which is what makes the strips of colour appear. A rainbow is actually a full circle, but you can't see the whole effect because of the horizon.

4. *Where do flies go in winter?*

Mature flies don't often survive the winter as they are thwarted in their efforts to hibernate by a tendency to come out as soon as there's a mild day, leading to almost certain death as soon as there's another cold snap. The eggs laid by a fly can stay in the pupae through the whole winter though, not emerging until the spring.

5. *What is a burp?*

A burp is a release of gas from the stomach or oesophagus. The gas gets there as a result of air being sucked down when drinking or eating, or it may come from the carbon dioxide bubbles in carbonated drinks. The sound that accompanies the burp is actually the vibration of the oesophagal sphincter as the gas passes through.

6. *Where do bogeys come from?*

Bogeys are formed from the mucus that our bodies produce to protect our lungs and respiratory system. When mucus, dust and dirt get mixed together in the nasal passage they solidify and produce bogeys. They contain a lot of bacteria and so it's really not a good idea to eat them.

7. *Why is there salt in the sea?*

There is salt in the sea because sea water comes into contact with land every time it evaporates. It is carried over-land in a cloud and then dumped as rain before flowing along rivers back into the sea. Salt and mineral deposits are rubbed away from the land during every cycle and that means the sea is salty and getting saltier. It also explains why the saltiest sea is the one with the smallest freshwater inlet and the greatest evaporation – the Red Sea.

8. **What happens when we die?**

This is a tricky question, but it's also a very personal question. If you have a religious belief, it can be hard to explain the complexities of an omniscient god to a four-year-old. Again, there may be a bit of hedging to be done. For example, it's perfectly reasonable to say that when we die we don't need our bodies anymore so they are turned into ashes or put into the ground where they slowly become part of the earth. This is a physical process which kids see all the time – effectively it's part of the recycling process. Keep this factual approach until your child is able to grasp more spiritual concepts.

9. **Why is 13 an unlucky number?**

The origins of 13 as an unlucky number are very old, and the exact origin is unclear, but the case for the poor unfortunate number wasn't helped by the presence of Judas as the 13th diner at the last supper. From this unlucky 13 the legend of 'Friday the 13th' has grown up, as has the reluctance on some builders' parts to name a house or flat 'number 13'. Other cultures without the Christian tradition have different lucky and unlucky numbers.

10. **What is the fastest animal?**

The fastest land animal is the cheetah, which can reach speeds of up to 80 miles per hour. It's not as fast as the swallow though, which can exceed 100 miles per hour.

Pocket fact

80% of parents have been stumped by their children's questions, according to a survey by Tickbox. The most common answer is, 'Ask your father/mother'.

3

THE LATER YEARS: TEENAGERS

Youth would be an ideal state if it came a little later in life.
Herbert Asquith

PASSING ON NEW SKILLS

Forget toddler tantrums: the truly tricky period of parenting comes around when your offspring reach their teens. This is the time when communication comes in the form of grunts and snarls and real life looms out of the shadows, threatening to take away your precious child's innocence. But it's not all doom and gloom – there are still a lot of things you'll be needed for and skills you can teach. With a bit of thought, planning and the wisdom that you'll find in the following chapter, you'll get through it just fine.

Teach your teen to . . . drive a car

Teaching teenagers to drive can be hard work – you need to be well prepared and extremely patient – but time behind the wheel with you by their side can be hugely beneficial, even if they are also taking more formal lessons with a qualified instructor. You can help your child in the following ways.

Show and tell

The first step in the process, long before you let your teen loose on the family saloon, is to talk them through a journey with you in the driving seat. Give them a guided tour of the car so that they understand the vocabulary you'll be using when it comes to the lessons proper. Then give an 'audio commentary' of a drive in the car, explaining exactly what you're doing and when – as well as pointing out things of note outside the car, like obstructions, signs and potential hazards.

Get legal

Before you start the lessons, make sure your teen has a provisional driving licence. You can get forms through the post office or via DVLA (www.dft.gov.uk/dvla/).

Start simple

Driving is all about confidence, so you need to start with a straightforward driving environment. A car park or industrial estate is a good place to practice – head out early in the morning on a Sunday to ensure you're undisturbed. This will give your teen the chance to get used to the controls and to manoeuvring the car without the distractions of other motorists.

Keep your cool

Don't allow conflict to creep into your sessions, no matter how dangerously they may be driving. You are the teacher, so you need to create a good, calm learning environment. This may involve biting your lip frequently, but it certainly means you should never raise your voice or try to take over driving. Keep it calm but professional.

Be upbeat

Even if progress is slow, the more you can encourage and reward responsible behaviour at this stage, the more likely it is that this behaviour will become second-nature. That means ending each session with a promise of more time, or perhaps ramping up slowly to more challenging driving conditions.

Pocket fact

Anyone who is over 21, has held a full driving licence for at least 3 years and is insured on the car can teach someone else to drive.

Teach your teen to . . . shave

Sure, shaving is instinctive now, but remember what it was like when you were starting out? Think horror movies and then add a dash more blood. Here's how to make the whole process painless for your son:

Wet shave, dry run

Even if you use an electric razor he'll probably be starting with a manual, so take him through a wet shave slowly and methodically, so that he can see what you do and has a decent model to copy. Just in case you need a boost, the perfect shave is outlined below:

1. **Wet means wet**. It's good practice to shave after a bath or shower, as the skin is nice and soft and relaxed. Wet the face thoroughly – using an exfoliating scrub if preferred.

2. **Lather up**. Work an inch or so of shaving gel on to your fingers and rub it into your beard. Don't overdo the gel: apply just enough to cover the beard growth area.

3. **Start sharp**. It's tempting to go for the cheapest disposable razors for practice but these will cut your boy's soft skin to ribbons. Instead, go for a decent quality multi-bladed brand, and make sure it's a new, sharp blade.

4. **Strokes of genius**. Sweep the razor down in gentle strokes, running *with* the grain of hair growth, *never* against it. Rinse the razor after each stroke to clear the hair from the blades.

5. **Cut throat business**. Take extra care around the neck and Adam's apple. The skin is thin and sensitive here, so don't be tempted to keep going over it – one gentle stroke will do it.

6. **Rinse and inspect**. Douse your face with cool water and inspect to see if you've missed anything.

7. **Stay cool**. Moisturise your skin after shaving to reduce shaving burn. Don't use aftershave at this stage – he's probably not ready for the sting!

When should your teen start shaving?

As soon as his facial hair becomes noticeable, or as soon as he wants to (and has some facial hair to shave). Most boys only need to shave sections of their face in the first year of shaving. Most boys start shaving around age 14 or 15. It varies enormously from person to person though.

Teach your teen to . . . tie a tie (and bowtie)

Teaching someone to tie a tie is a little like teaching them to shave – it's fine to give plenty of demonstrations but eventually they will just need to get on with practising themselves. Tying a tie is a pretty standard procedure once perfected; a bowtie can be much fiddlier. Here's a simple guide to both:

The tie

- Raise the collar of your shirt and drape the tie around your neck, with the wide end hanging down approximately twice as low as the narrow end.

- Take the wide end and wrap it twice around the narrow end just under your chin.

- Now feed the wide end up and through the gap between the knot and your chin, bringing it down and back through the loop created at the front of the knot.

- Pull both wide and narrow ends of the tie until the knot is secure. Make sure the ends hang ok – otherwise you'll have to start again, adjusting the lengths accordingly.

- Flip your collar back down and you're ready to impress.

The bowtie

- Place the tie around you neck so that one end is about 4cm longer than the other.

- Fold the shorter end and hold it in a bow-shape across your neckline. Then loop the long end over and in front of this bow so it hangs down at right angles.

- Loop the longer bow back up behind the short section, then fold the long part into another bow to look the same as the first.

- Rotate this second bow 180 degrees and slide it through the loop in front of the first bow.

- Straighten and adjust the tie to fit. It takes a bit of practice to perfect, but it does look much better than a ready-made bowtie.

Teach your teen to . . . attend a job interview

It may have been a while since your last job interview, but that doesn't mean basic interview techniques have changed. You can help your teen prepare for an important interview in a number of ways.

Teach the basics

Whatever the job, your teen will need to be aware of some fundamentals – good presentation is key, which means being dressed well, punctual, polite and alert. They should do some homework on the company before they arrive at the interview and they should make sure they are very familiar with the CV or application form they submitted just in case any specific questions are asked in relation to it.

Practice makes perfect

Do a dummy-run of the interview, or preferably use a family friend with a good objective manner and experience of interviewing. Simulate the entire interview process – from the handshake and greeting to the background questions, through to your teen's opportunity to ask questions of the interviewer – this is often where the really strong candidate shines. Ask your friend to look out for areas that can be improved, especially taking into account manner, body language and eye contact. These non-verbal means of communication have a massive impact on the impression we give at interviews. When you give your teen feedback, always start with the positives before offering any criticisms.

Follow up with constructive comments

However your child tells you the interview went, look for the positives. If they are not successful, advise them to ask for feedback so they know what they can improve. Often feedback is actually good for someone's confidence, as it often contains a lot of positive points, as well as a few constructive criticisms.

Pocket fact 🔔

The best job in the world is believed to be the role of caretaker of Hamilton Island, Queensland, Australia. The job was filled by

Ben Southall from Hampshire, UK, who beat a field of 34,000 applicants for the £70,000+ per annum role.

🚗 DEALING WITH A TEEN 🚗

Although it looks like one long festival of lie-ins, parties and free love, a typical teenager's life is actually pretty angst-ridden. Aside from the physical changes that a teenager goes through in puberty, there's the emotional upheaval of love, sex, political and social awareness and even the stress of actually getting a decent education to factor in.

So it's not really surprising that teens can get pretty stressed on occasions. Mood swings and emotional outbursts are fairly common and while you shouldn't run to the nearest anger management expert every time an argument blows up, you do need to be careful that frustration doesn't spill over into more serious emotional problems. Here are some tips to help you keep a lid on tensions.

Recognise the signs

If you have flashpoints over certain issues – staying out late, cleaning up or doing chores – don't raise these issues when either of you is tired. The argument will quickly spiral into name-calling and will just create further distance between you.

Sum it up

When you do have a problem to discuss, hold a meeting with your teen to discuss it sensibly – at a time that's convenient to you both. Be prepared to hear your teen's opinion and make it clear that you are prepared to have a debate – but your word will be final.

Chill

Everyone benefits from periods of calm, and if you can encourage your teen to share in some relaxing pursuits when things are going well – listening to music, breathing exercises, even sports like swimming or boxing – these same techniques will help them when there's tension around.

Be realistic

Your teen is going through the same life changes that affected you – and your own parents – at the same age. Be philosophical if he or she won't speak to you or is constantly at odds with you. You represent authority and that's a bad thing for teens. As long as you are there when they need you and don't make the mistake of trying too hard to be hip, you'll get through this stage with your relationship intact.

Ten bands even your teen will think are cool

1. *The Beatles*
2. *The Rolling Stones*
3. *Led Zeppelin*
4. *The Who*
5. *Velvet Underground*
6. *The Ramones*
7. *Pink Floyd*
8. *The Kinks*
9. *Bob Marley and the Wailers*
10. *The Clash*

HOUSE PARTIES

Whatever you and your partner are to your teenage child, you are not their ideal social network. They want to be with their friends and well away from you – that's fine and natural but you still need to be in control, especially with early teens.

For older children, house parties become increasingly popular. If you're brave enough to hold one, you'll need a few ground rules.

Master of the house

In exchange for hiding yourself away in the bedroom for the whole evening, you will need a show of respect for your property – that means no breakages, no mixed sex sleepovers, no alcohol and enough peace and quiet to ensure the other occupants of the house (and the neighbourhood) get enough sleep.

Managing numbers

Set a strict limit on the number of people your child's allowed to invite. Make them aware that you are available to help if there are gate crashers, or if it gets out of hand.

Booze and teens

Be very clear about your policy on alcohol from the start. If you know there's alcohol at the party when you have banned it, first take your child to one side and ask them to explain your policy to their friends. Don't fly off the handle straight away, but also don't be afraid to enforce your policy. It's your house after all!

Pocket tip 🍺

When your teen is out and about with friends, make sure they have a mobile phone with your mobile and home numbers on speed dial and enough credit to call you anytime. Teen parties can get out of hand, and if they are away from home you need to know you can get to them quickly.

SLEEPOVERS

Sleepovers are a great way for kids to socialise, and are really popular amongst teenage girls.

Contact numbers

Make sure you have the home contact details of everyone who is involved in the sleepover. While they are in your house, they are your responsibility and you need to know whom to call if there's an emergency.

Leave them be

If you've agreed to a sleepover, don't disturb them unless it is really necessary. If there's too much noise, get your partner to act as the go-between, keeping yourself well out of the picture.

ALCOHOL AND DRUGS

What to do if your child . . . gets drunk

Your reaction to drunkenness should be based on a variety of factors: the age of your child; how often they are drinking; where and when they are drinking; and your own experience of and attitude to alcohol.

How young is too young?

You can take the pious approach and say that children under 18 should never buy any alcohol, either in a pub or from a shop. But while that's the letter of the law, the spirit (pardon the pun) is very different. Most 16-year-olds don't go to youth clubs to play ping pong and sip orange squash: they go to pubs and they drink alcohol (or at least they'll try their damned hardest to). At this age, your best bet is education rather than control. Make sure your child is aware of the damage that excessive alcohol consumption can do to their body and to their bank balance.

How much is too much?

As mentioned above, you need to assess the impact of alcohol use on your child's life in general. While drinking and socialising with friends is a major part of teen life, it can rapidly become a habit that leads to loss of concentration and failing standards at school, as well as underlying health problems. It might be better to set some loose boundaries – allow them to have a drink on a Friday or Saturday night, but never in the week. You may witness the occasional binge (and the resultant hangover) but this doesn't mean there's a problem – your teen is probably learning more from the odd excess than you could ever teach them by imposing a ban.

Where to go?

They might want to go to the pub to drink, but they are breaking the law if they do – plus there is the added complication of transport: if someone drives they must be aware of the dangers of drunk driving. Encourage them to have a couple of friends round and get the (mid-strength) beers in yourself. This helps you monitor their alcohol consumption, but it also gives them somewhere safe and legal to socialise.

Pocket fact 🍶

It is illegal to give alcohol to a child of four and under, unless you are under professional supervision in a medical emergency. You can buy alcohol in your own home for any child above this age. Children may go to a pub under the age of 16, but certain restrictions may apply and they cannot drink alcohol. Children of 16 years and over may drink wine, beer or cider with a pub or restaurant meal if the drink is purchased by an adult.

What to do if your child . . . takes drugs

A recent survey suggested that up to one third of teenagers have experimented with drugs by the age of 15. That sounds like a pretty stark statistic until you focus on the word 'experiment'. Teens experiment, that's what they do. The key is to be alert enough to spot the signs that your teen has moved from experiment to abuse. Signs of sustained drug use include the following:

● Listlessness, tiredness, lack of interest and appetite
● Red-rimmed eyes and running nose
● Aggression, mood swings and general behavioural changes
● Altered sleep pattern – bouts of insomnia or inability to wake up
● Theft of money or personal possessions
● Defensive and secretive behaviour
● Deterioration of personal interests

Of course, many of these signs could also be an indication of something else – an illness, a bout of depression caused by other factors, or even just teen hormonal changes – but taken together, or sustained over a long period, they should be checked out. You need to do this through gentle discussion: tell your teen that you are free to talk at any time and that you can help them if they need anything from you. The less they see you as someone to hide from, the more likely you are to get a positive reaction. Do your own research into drugs and make sure you talk openly within the family about the subject. Then if it ever becomes a problem, everyone is aware that help is at hand. Try Frank, the UK's national anti-drug campaign (www.talktofrank.com).

TEENAGERS AND SEX

Teach your teen . . . safe sex

Sex is an embarrassing subject for most people – it would be great if it weren't, but it is. It's this embarrassment, and the associated giggling, that has given the UK such a massive teen pregnancy rate. We simply don't talk enough about what not to do. Here's how to make sure your teens don't become another statistic.

The facts

Don't wait to be asked about the facts of life. After a youthful 'where do babies come from?', kids don't speak to their parents about sex: they speak to their friends, and that's where myth turns into fact. Make sure your teen is fully aware of the facts by asking what they know – and don't rely on euphemisms: name the sex organs and don't leave anything open to misunderstanding.

The good bits

Telling your teen that sex is the root of all evil is the quickest way to get them jumping into the sack with the next likely candidate. Explain that sex is a positive physical and emotional experience – especially when it is shared with someone you love and respect.

The bad bits

Explain the realities of pregnancy and of sexually transmitted diseases. The more open and clear you are, the more likely your teen is to come to you with any questions or concerns.

Talk safety

Acknowledge the fact that your child will ultimately want to experiment when the time is right, but talk about contraception.

Explain that you will be happy to talk to them if they want to make a choice about contraception – you may think they're too young, but you won't be able to stop them.

Answer openly

Give open and frank answers to any questions your teen may have. If you don't know all the answers, take a look at the NHS website together for information on sexual health (www.nhs.uk/LiveWell/sexualhealth).

PREGNANCY

What to do if your child . . . gets pregnant

Stay calm. Inside your mind right now you are probably contemplating buying a shotgun and going to find the father-to-be, but anger and confrontation will not help – in fact, you will just drive your daughter away, limiting her choices into the bargain.

Instead you need to consider *her* choices and the practicalities of the situation. There are some things she needs to do alone and others that you can help with.

She must:

● Visit the doctor to confirm the pregnancy and discuss her options.

You must:

● Be open and ready to discuss all available options (keeping the baby, abortion, adoption).

● Give her support and emotional strength.

● Do your homework – figure out the realities and practicalities of all the alternatives and help her reach her own informed decision.

What to do if your child . . . gets a girl pregnant

If you're on the other side of the equation and your son has got a girl pregnant, you need to face the same practicalities as if it were your daughter. There is a financial and social responsibility in fatherhood and your son needs to know his options – so you need to help him research these.

He has a right to express his opinion, but ultimately the girl has the right to decide the outcome of the pregnancy. You may want to meet the girl's parents to discuss their approach – do this by letter initially, offering your support and input. Don't be offended if they reject your offer – they are simply trying to cope in their own way.

Top five coolest dads in the world

1. **David Beckham**. *Despite the comedy helium accent, Beckham is the archetypal 'cool' dad. He is fantastically rich without a great deal of effort and everyone respects him.*
2. **Andrew 'Freddie' Flintoff**. *There's something about Fred that makes him really cool as a dad, even though by his own admission he doesn't change that many nappies. He's an old school dad with a slightly roguish air.*
3. **Brad Pitt**. *He just looks great. Git.*
4. **Jamie Oliver**. *Cool because he can do stuff really well. Jamie Oliver gives the impression of being a genuinely likeable guy, which could just be an act, in which case he's also a brilliant actor.*
5. **Homer Simpson**. *Cool for all the wrong reasons. Homer is the little voice in your head that you should ignore. Think of great Homer quotes, such as: 'I'd do anything for you Lisa, especially if it's easy' and, 'Kids, you tried your best and failed miserably. The lesson is, never try.'*

🚗 **RECKLESS BEHAVIOUR** 🚗

What to do if your child . . . gets in a fight

Your reaction to your child is a vital factor in how they will deal with the aftermath. If you are told by the school or even by the police about the fight, don't overreact and apportion blame before you understand the facts of the situation. There are always two participants in a fight, so the chances of your child being blameless are slim. You need to understand the causes and see what can be done to stop it happening again. So calmly talk to your child, explaining that there's no blame and no punishment. If they are able to tell you the truth, explain that you're disappointed that they couldn't think of a better way to solve the problem and suggest ways they could have avoided the conflict.

Pocket tip 🍺

A parent's disappointment is a lot harder to bear than anger.

What to do if your child . . . steals

At home

If you child steals from you, don't overreact. Stealing is a classic cry for help and children are often caught out because they want to be. With careful handling and an atmosphere of debate rather than blame, you can hopefully get to the root to the problem – which may be something totally unconnected with the stolen item.

In public

If your child steals from a shop, it is unlikely that they will face a trip to court – though custodial sentences are possible in certain aggravated theft cases. They are more likely to face an on-the-spot fine from the police. The humiliation of a trip in a police car and the knowledge that you will probably have to 'bail them out' will be enough for the experience to linger long in the memory. Control your own anger and calmly talk about why they stole. Make sure any punishment you give them doesn't simply drive them to commit more crime – ie don't take away their allowance.

What to do if your child . . . gets fired

At the risk of sounding like a stuck record, the key here is to stay relaxed about the situation and try to get an idea of the underlying causes. If your child was sacked from a job for doing it badly, for laziness, or incompetence, these are undoubtedly negative things, but they are life lessons — your child will lose wages that could have been spent on socialising and buying nice things, which may well be punishment enough. Part-time or weekend jobs have pretty relaxed conditions, so a sacking isn't going to ruin your child's career. If the sacking is a result of theft or gross misconduct, this is a more serious issue — but again, the way you react should be linked to the action that caused the sacking, not the sacking itself.

The thankless position of the father in the family — the provider for all, the enemy of all.
August Strindberg

Pocket fact 🔖

The world's youngest dad is believed to be Alfie Patten who became a father at age 13.

4

THE HUNTER-GATHERER: FOOD AND DRINK

There are few virtues a man can possess more erotic than culinary skill.
Isabel Allende

Gone are the days when men burnt salads and lived off beans from the can – we have an equal right to the kitchen and most men do at least know their way around a cookery book, thanks to macho kitchen role models such as Gordon Ramsay. So how do you get to cook like Gordon without swearing like him as the heat cranks up? Follow these fantastic culinary tips and recipes for a foolproof way to kitchen mastery.

🚗 SEVEN CHILD-FRIENDLY 🚗 RECIPES ALL DADS SHOULD KNOW

EASY SPAGHETTI BOLOGNESE

Any pasta dish (especially whole wheat pasta) will give your child a filling and nutritious meal. The secret is in avoiding a high salt content jar of pasta sauce. Instead go for a simple jar of passata or can of chopped tomatoes, and add some roughly chopped basil, a little pepper and some diced onion.

1. Fry the onion and 1 lb of beef mince until it is browned all over and then add the other ingredients to make the sauce, making sure to drain away any excess fat from the minced beef first. Leave the sauce to simmer for 20 minutes.

2. While your sauce is simmering, cook the pasta according to the manufacturer's instructions. Fresh pasta needs just 2-5 minutes to cook on average, whereas dried pasta needs

around 10-12 minutes. If you are cooking spaghetti, break the pasta in two as this will make it easier for little people to eat.

3. Serve with a sprinkling of grated mild cheese – a Cheddar or Cheshire cheese is ideal. That's a whole meal cooked inside 25 minutes.

BACON AND BEANS ON TOAST

This is just about the ideal breakfast, but it makes a pretty good evening meal as well. The trick is to use smoked streaky bacon.

1. Fry the bacon, then leave to rest on a sheet of kitchen towel before cutting into very thin slices.

2. Warm a can of low-salt baked beans on a low heat on the hob and add the bacon, stirring frequently.

3. Toast some wholemeal bread, spread with a light margarine and cut into 2cm squares.

4. Pour the bacon and beans over the top and serve with a glug of brown sauce.

DO-IT-YOURSELF PIZZAS

1. Buy some pizza bases from the supermarket (it's as cheap as making them, honestly), and chop some onions, peppers and mushrooms into fine slices.

2. Grate some cheese and shred some ham, or slice salami thinly. You can also add in olives, pineapple chunks, chicken or tuna, depending on your child's tastes.

3. Put all the ingredients into separate dishes and let them run wild, starting with a tomato base and ending up with a sprinkling of cheese to top it off.

4. Encourage them to be creative, make shapes or pictures with the ingredients. The more they get involved, the more likely they are to eat the end product.

5. Place the finished pizzas on the middle shelf of a pre-heated oven at 190°C (gas mark 5) for 10–12 minutes.

This 'do-it-yourself' principle for kids also works well with fajitas and baked potatoes.

Pocket tip 🍺

You can avoid crying while peeling onions if you chew some gum or a long-lasting toffee. You could also try peeling it under water (the onion, not you).

COTTAGE PIE

1. Follow the instructions outlined above for the Bolognese sauce, but add thin slices of carrot and a beef stock cube to the sauce.

2. Peel, chop and boil some potatoes for at least 15 minutes or until they are very soft. Drain off the water, add a splash of milk and a knob of low-fat spread, then mash thoroughly.

3. Put the mince and sauce in the bottom of an ovenproof dish and then cover with the mashed potato.

4. Top this with some grated cheese and cook on a medium heat in the oven for about 35–40 minutes at 180°C (gas mark 4). Serve with steamed vegetables.

CHICKEN/FISH STIR-FRY

This is another simple and quick weekday favourite. You will need some sliced chicken breast or fresh prawns, some sliced button mushrooms, diced peppers, diced onions and some slivers of carrot. You'll also need some noodles, which can be boiled if they're dry or simply stirred in with the other ingredients if they're fresh.

1. First heat a little olive oil on a medium heat and then fry the strips of chicken until they are browned.

2. Add the vegetables and a decent slosh of light soy sauce and stir for a couple of minutes.

3. Finally, mix in the noodles and serve straight away.

A CURRY FOR ALL TASTES

This is a simple chicken curry that can be cooked slowly and it's mild enough for the whole family to enjoy. You will need: a large onion (sliced), some curry spices (1 tsp of turmeric, crushed cumin, crushed fennel, paprika, ¼ tsp of cinnamon), 250ml of chicken stock, three large chicken breasts (cubed), 1tsp of sugar, 2tbsp of tomato puree and about 50ml of cream.

1. Fry the chicken and the onion in a little butter until browned, then add all the other ingredients except the cream.

2. Allow the curry to cook for a couple of hours to really bring out the flavours and add the cream just before serving.

3. Serve with rice or naan bread.

ROAST CHICKEN WITH ALL THE TRIMMINGS

Nothing beats a roast dinner, and no roast beats chicken, so if you can master this dish, you can keep the whole family happy. The trick is in the timing so watch this like a hawk . . .

1. First wash the chicken. Stuff it with an apple to give it some extra moisture and rub the skin with olive oil. Put it in the oven at 190°C (gas mark 5) (a little lower in a fan oven) for 20 minutes per 500g plus a further 20 minutes. An average-sized bird takes about two hours.

2. After half an hour or so, peel some potatoes and put them in boiling water for about 10 minutes. They don't need to be soft. Drain them and give them a good shake in the saucepan. Add the potatoes to the roasting tin with the chicken and baste them with more olive oil.

3. Allow the potatoes and chicken to cook together for another hour or so, occasionally basting and turning the potatoes.

4. Wrap some streaky bacon around mini sausages, put them on a lightly oiled baking tray and add them to the oven. Then prepare and steam some vegetables.

5. Take the chicken out of the oven 10 minutes before everything else is ready, drain off some of the fat into your gravy powder to make a nice juicy mix and leave the chicken to one side.

6. Carve or quarter the chicken and serve with all the accompaniments.

7. Sit back and wait for the praise.

How to . . . bake a Victoria sponge

Particularly helpful around Mother's Day, this recipe is simple and works (nearly) every time.

1. Weigh three large eggs (with shell on) and measure out exactly the same amount of margarine, self-raising flour and caster sugar.

2. Preheat the oven to 180°C (gas mark 4).

3. Cream together the margarine and sugar either by hand or in a food processor until the mixture is pale and fluffy.

4. Add the eggs and 1tbsp of the flour to prevent curdling.

5. Fold in the flour and 1tsp of baking powder.

6. Divide the mixture between two lined 20cm cake tins.

7. Bake on the middle shelf for 30–35 minutes or until the centre of the cake springs back when pressed lightly (check without removing the cake from the oven).

8. Turn out of the tin and allow to cool. Sandwich the two halves together, base to base, using the very best raspberry jam and sprinkle icing sugar on top.

Pocket tip 🍺

For a quick method of lining a cake tin, cut a square of baking parchment roughly wider than the cake tin. Fold in half, then half and half again. Cut the outside corner in a circular shape. Unfold and place in the tin. There is no need to grease the tin as well.

How to . . . make pancakes

1. Sift 110g of plain flour with a pinch of salt.

2. Make a well in the centre of the flour and break two eggs into it. Whisk the eggs, folding in the flour.

3. Gradually incorporate 200ml of milk and 1tbsp of sunflower oil, whisking until the batter is smooth.

4. Leave the batter to stand for one hour.

5. Heat a small frying-pan until it is very hot, then turn the heat down to medium. Ladle in about 2tbsp of the batter. Tip it from side to side so that the pan is evenly coated. Cook for about 30 seconds until the bottom is golden. Flip the pancake using a palette knife, then slide it out of the pan onto a plate.

6. Stack the pancakes between sheets of greaseproof paper to keep warm while making the rest.

🚗 HEALTHY TREATS FOR 🚗 HUNGRY KIDS

Snack food doesn't mean unhealthy food. Kids are at their best when they're eating something that's presented in an interesting and fun way. Here are some examples.

A mess of tortilla chips

Get some unsalted tortilla chips, smother them in salsa, guacamole and cheese, then bake in the oven for 25 minutes at 180°C (gas mark 4). Result – a sticky mess and some happy kids.

Cracker faces

Some large crackers, blocks of cheese, chopped cherry tomatoes and some soft cheese spread go together to make a funny-faced easy treat.

Tempura vegetables

Mix up a tempura batter (a simple combination of 50g cornflower, 50g plain flour, 250ml cold water, 1 ½tsp baking powder and an egg) and dip broccoli and cauliflower florets (little trees) and carrot sticks into the batter. Shallow fry in a little hot vegetable oil, turning while cooking. Serve with a tomato ketchup dip.

Toast shapes

Toast is a great standby, especially if the kids are hungry after school. You can make it more interesting by using a shape stamp to make interesting shapes in the buttered toast.

Dried fruit and nuts

Older children love nuts and fruit. Buy some big packs from a health food shop and put them in a couple of storage jars. Then, when the children fancy a snack, you can get them to add the fruit and nuts to a bowl of whole-wheat cereal.

Pocket fact

A human being can live without food for a month, but only for a few days without water. If the body's water level gets reduced by 10% it is fatal. One of the key signs of extreme dehydration is a lack of thirst, as the thirst instinct shuts down.

How to . . . host the perfect barbecue

We all know that the barbecue is the preserve of the father, but few of us seem to be aware that barbecued food involves anything more than a stack of charred sausages and a half-cooked chicken drumstick. With a bit of preparation and a decent spell of weather, you can turn the barbecue into a centre of culinary excellence.

Pocket tip 🍺

Light the barbecue about half an hour before you want to cook anything, and don't put any meat on until there are no flames and the coals are grey. To improve the flavour of the meat, lay some herbs such as rosemary on the coals of the barbecue. Kettle barbecues are great for all-round cooking as they allow you to cook much more slowly.

- Fish is a great option on a barbecue. Wrap a salmon fillet, some herbs and butter in some kitchen foil and place onto the grill alongside your meat. The fish will gently steam in the foil but will also have a faintly smoky flavour.

- Shish kebabs are also good barbecue options. Put diced chicken, cherry tomatoes, halved button mushrooms and sliced peppers on metal skewers and cook them either as they are or coated in a marinade of soy sauce mixed with sugar, herbs and vegetable oil.

- Take some medium-sized potatoes, prick the skins with a fork, wrap them in foil and place them in the coals of the barbecue. After an hour or so, they'll be ready to eat.

Pocket fact ⚱

1.2 billion people in the world are underfed. Exactly the same number are overweight.

Top tips in the kitchen
- *Always your wash hands with soap or antibacterial liquid before you touch any foodstuffs.*

- *Keep raw meat on a lower shelf of the fridge than cooked meats or vegetables. Seal raw meats in a tight container to keep blood and other juices from getting out into the fridge.*
- *If you're cutting meat, make sure you use a plastic chopping board and wash it – and the knife – thoroughly before you cut any other foods such as vegetables.*
- *If you're using meat or fish from the freezer, make sure they are completely defrosted before you begin cooking.*
- *If you're cooking anything in the microwave, stop midway through the cooking time and give it a good stir to ensure the food is cooked evenly.*
- *Cook all meat and fish until they are piping hot. If you're feeding children, avoid serving rare meat, even if you know it is from a reliable source, as children are much more susceptible to food poisoning.*

🚗 COOKING WITH CHILDREN 🚗

Yes, we all know the old one about cooking with children, but this is not a wicked witch's fantasy: this is a real opportunity for you to pass on a skill to your young ones. *And* you might learn a bit yourself. Getting your children involved in the kitchen from an early age will teach them good habits and means they are less likely to be fussy eaters.

When you're teaching kids to cook, start simple.

FALAFEL

Makes about eight balls

1. Blend one 400g can of chickpeas, drained and rinsed, in a food processor until smooth.

2. Add one crushed clove of garlic, 1tbsp each of chopped fresh parsley and mint, 1tsp of ground cumin, zest of half a lemon, 1tbsp of lemon juice, and 2tbsp of fresh breadcrumbs. Mix well.

3. Form into balls using hands, pressing the mixture so that it sticks together.

4. Place in the fridge for 30 minutes to firm up.

5. Shallow fry a few falafels at a time in oil, for about 10 minutes or until golden.

6. Serve in pitta bread with salad and Greek yoghurt, though children may prefer them dipped in tomato ketchup.

ALL-IN-ONE CUPCAKES

Makes 12 cakes

1. Combine two eggs, 125g of self-raising flour, 125g of butter, 125g of caster sugar, and 1tsp of vanilla essence in a bowl. Beat until smooth.

2. Fill 12 cupcake cases and bake for 18–20 minutes in an oven preheated to 180°C (gas mark 4), until the cakes are firm and golden.

3. Ice and decorate with a selection of the following: silver balls, dragées, glace cherries, sprinkles, mini-marshmallows, liquorice laces, and jelly beans. Try making animal faces (pigs, mice, cats), insects (caterpillars, spiders, butterflies) or flowers.

CHOCOLATE CRISPIE CAKES

Makes 12 cakes

1. Place 200g good quality chocolate, broken into pieces, with 1tbsp of butter and 1tsp of golden syrup in a heatproof bowl.

2. Place the bowl on top of a saucepan of barely simmering water (make sure the bowl does not touch the bottom of the pan)

3. Alternatively, heat the bowl in the microwave for two to three minutes, in short 30-second bursts, stirring each time. When almost fully melted, stir well until smooth.

4. Remove the bowl from the heat and add 100g cornflakes, stirring until they are all coated.

5. Place a heaped tbsp of the mixture into each paper case and refrigerate until set.

6. Experiment by adding different types of cereal, dried fruit, mini-marshmallows etc. Substitute dark or white chocolate for a more sophisticated or sweeter flavour.

🚗 CONVERSION CHART 🚗

The measurements and conversions given below are approximate:

Ounces/lbs	Grams	Ounces/lbs	Grams
¼oz	5g	9oz	225g
½oz	10g	10oz	250g
1oz	25g	11oz	275g
2oz	50g	12oz	300g
3oz	75g	13oz	325g
4oz	100g	14oz	350g
5oz	125g	15oz	375g
6oz	150g	1lb	400g
7oz	175g	1½lb	700g
8oz	200g	2lb	900g

Pints	ml/litres
¼ pt	125ml
½ pt	250ml
¾ pt	375ml
1 pt	500ml
1½ pt	750ml
2 pt	1 litre

Spoons	ml
1 teaspoon	5ml
1 dessertspoon	10ml
1 tablespoon	15ml

🚗 FOOD TERMINOLOGY EXPLAINED 🚗

The following is a glossary of key cooking language as used in recipe books.

Al dente. A term used to describe food – especially pasta and vegetables – which is soft on the outside but has a firmness in the middle.

Baste. This is the process (usually while roasting meat) of covering something with its own juices while it is cooking.

Cream. Beating fat or butter with sugar to make a light, fluffy mixture.

Flake. Separating food into its natural parts using a fork – usually refers to fish.

Fold. Gently mixing ingredients, usually including an egg white, with a metal spoon so that the ingredients don't lose their lightness.

Gratin. Any dish that is topped with grated cheese, butter and sometimes breadcrumbs as well.

Julienne. Cutting vegetables (such as carrots) into evenly sliced fine strips so that they look nice and cook quickly. Good for making raw carrot snacks.

Marinade. To leave food (particularly meat) in a flavoured liquid for a long time so that it takes on the flavour of the liquid.

Prick. It's not what you think – this is what you must do to the skin of vegetables and fruit before baking to stop them bursting during cooking. Think of baked potatoes and baked apples.

Purée. To blend or mash something until it is smooth.

Reduce. To boil a liquid so that you make it into a more concentrated form.

Roux. A mixture of flour and fat (or butter), cooked slowly over a gentle heat. This is the basis for many sauces and soups.

Simmer. To cook something on a hob just below boiling point. The water should move but not bubble when the pan is simmering.

Stock. The liquid created when something is simmered for a long time.

Sweat. To cook something (usually a vegetable such as leeks or an onion) in a little oil or fat over medium to low heat in a pan with the lid on. The first step in making decent vegetable soup is to sweat the onions.

🚗 DRINKS FOR KIDS 🚗

ICE CREAM SMOOTHIE

Drinks don't have to be full of sugar to be fun. The advent of the smoothie bar makes it much more acceptable to drink healthily and, with a little bit of preparation, you can knock up your own smoothies easily.

You need: three scoops of vanilla ice cream, a quarter of a pint of milk, sliced banana, a handful of strawberries, the juice of a couple of oranges and a spoonful of honey.

1. Place all the ingredients in a blender and mix well.

2. Switch off the power and use a wooden spoon to mix around the smoothie to make sure all the big lumps have disappeared. Mix again if necessary.

3. If the smoothie is too thick, add more milk to the mixture. Serve in a long glass with a thick straw.

You can use the same process (minus the ice cream) to make great healthy milkshakes for kids. You can even get them to combine their own ingredients – melon, mango, raspberries and peeled peaches all make great smoothie ingredients.

Pocket tip 🍺
If ice cream is too cold to serve, put the serving spoon into a mug of boiling water first, leave it for a minute and then try again.

HOMEMADE LEMONADE

Heat 225g of sugar and 300g of water in a saucepan until boiling. Remove from heat and allow to cool while stirring to dissolve all the sugar. Use this mixture as the basis for the lemonade – you'll only need a couple of tablespoons per glass but don't worry as the sugar solution will keep under wraps in the fridge for weeks. Mix 2tbsp of this sugar solution with the juice of half a lemon and half a pint of cold water to make the perfect glass of still lemonade.

HOMEMADE BARLEY WATER

To make enough barley water for four thirsty kids, take 200g pearl barley, rinsed in hot water, and then boil it up with the rind of four lemons and 4 pints of water. When this has boiled and simmered for 25 minutes, strain it through a sieve and add the juice of the lemons and a little sugar or honey to sweeten. Chill in the fridge before serving.

HOMEMADE ICE LOLLIES

When it's hot, a homemade lolly hits the spot perfectly – giving the kids some much-needed hydration and avoiding expensive and sugar-filled shop-bought alternatives. Simply juice an orange and mix with a little water in an ice lolly mould. Place in the freezer for a few hours to set and then enjoy.

Be content to remember that those who can make omelettes
properly can do nothing else.
Hilaire Belloc

5

EDUCATION

Nine tenths of education is encouragement.
Anatole France

Sending your children off to school can be a scary and daunting task: you need to make sure you choose a school that suits your child and will set them up for the best start in life. You also need to be able to support them throughout the whole of their education, from that first day at school to waving them off at university. This chapter will help those big days go smoothly and gives you tips on everything in between, from homework to making sure they're happy at school.

🚗 FIRST DAY – NOT WORST DAY 🚗

Your child's first day at school – primary or secondary – is a massive occasion. Whether the task of dropping your child off for the big day falls to you or your partner, here are a few pointers to help you encourage your child, and make sure they're organised.

PRIMARY SCHOOL

- Read some books with your child about the first day at school – talk about your own first day and the kind of things your child will see and do.

- Don't just brush your child's fears aside. Listen carefully to their worries and address them if you can.

- Make sure you know exactly where and when your child needs to be at the school on the first day. If it's a work day, try to be there for the drop off at least. Check to see if there is any documentation required when you register.

- Make sure you go to any open days that the school has – this will give you a chance to meet the teachers and see the facilities.

- Prepare your child for the big day by making sure they are able to dress themselves and manage trips to the toilet unaccompanied.

SECONDARY SCHOOL

- Make sure you are upbeat about the school, even if you've got your own concerns.

- Walk through the route to school with your child.

- Make sure your child has some money for emergencies, or credit on their phone if these are permitted in the school.

- If you can get hold of a timetable, look at it with your child and discuss any kit or other equipment that will be needed and on which days.

- Have some family time together at the beginning of the day to discuss the day ahead and to have a decent breakfast together. The breakfast will help your child's energy levels and the chat may just bring up anything needed for the school day that's been overlooked.

- Have another informal chat over dinner at the end of the day – you don't need an interrogation, just a show of interest.

- Let your child know that they are welcome to bring friends round after school or at weekends – this will help them to build friendships.

- Encourage participation in after-school clubs or activities, but make sure they don't become overburdened by extra-curricular activities.

🚗 HELPING WITH HOMEWORK 🚗

Helping a child with homework is a great way to spend some time together discussing the day, finding out if there are any problems at school and generally checking all is well.

- Don't be tempted to take over and find out the answers yourself. Instead, help your child to research the answers as fully as possible, only then guiding them to the right answer if necessary. Teaching then study skills will prepare them for life: giving them the answers won't prepare them for anything.

- Create a learning environment. You can help your child achieve more by providing a good environment for study – that means giving them a peaceful, well-lit, dedicated homework area, a computer of their own with internet access and a decent library of reference books.

- Be web wise. Make sure you've got effective parental controls on your child's web browser. The internet is also fast becoming the source of a lot of easy cut-and-paste homework activities. While you're signing the homework diary, you should be able to spot if the work looks 'borrowed' from the web.

Useful websites for homework help

www.topmarks.co.uk
www.learn.co.uk
www.maths.com
www.scholastic.co.uk
www.happychild.org.uk
www.underfives.co.uk
www.channel4learning.com/apps/homeworkhigh
www.bbc.co.uk/schools/parents

GETTING A TUTOR

A private tutor can provide great targeted help if your child has a particularly weak subject area. Before you hire someone, speak to your child's form teacher at school and explain what you are considering. They may be able to suggest areas to focus on, which will save you money in the long run. They may even have recommendations for you. When you do hire a tutor, try to get your child involved as much as possible – they need to be able to work with the tutor, so personality is important. You'll probably need to get the tutor to do sessions of one and a half to two hours once a week – expect to pay anything from £20 to £30 per hour depending on the subject.

Pocket tip 🍺

Tuition works best when it has a clear brief as well as a focus and an end result – such as an exam or qualification.

INTERNET SAFETY

The internet brings the whole world into your house. But the whole world is sometimes a pretty frightening place, and your child may need protecting from some of its worst excesses. It's hard to keep up to date with internet security as the technology changes so often. While you can manage access from your own computer, you can't control what your child sees at a friend's house or on a mobile. The best way to tackle internet abuse is to teach your child what is right and wrong from a young age, and to encourage responsible use of the web.

There are many things you can do to encourage responsible use:

- Make sure the computer is in a family room or shared-access space.

- Use an ISP (Internet Service Provider) with a family-friendly policy.

- Understand the enemy – take a look as a 'guest' around some popular chat rooms and social networking sites so that you can understand what goes on – and get familiar with the lingo.

- Make sure the chatrooms your child uses are effectively moderated.

- Be security conscious by installing a family-friendly internet safety package – including anti-spyware and anti-virus software.

- Keep an eye on your child's internet usage by limiting time online and checking their browsing history to ensure they haven't visited any suspect sites. Remember that browsing history can be deleted by the canny user, so you should also be suspicious if the history has been wiped.

- If you do discover that your child has visited any unsuitable sites, given out personal details or has done anything else that breaks your own rules, don't get angry as that will just make them hide their behaviour. Talk about the risks and the consequences of internet abuse instead.

Above all, make sure that your child is aware of the following rules:

- Never give out any personal information – name, age, address, school, bank details.

- Never send personal photos to another internet user.

- Never use a chatroom without the permission of an adult – especially if users can 'hide' behind false identities.

- If your child becomes the victim of cyber-bullying, don't reply to abusive emails or messages, and talk to your child to comfort them.

- Never open attachments unless they are from someone you know – and even then, don't open forwarded attachments sent to everyone from a friend's address book. It may contain a virus.

🚗 BULLYING 🚗

What to do if your child . . . gets bullied

Bullying is a terrible and often destructive blight on childhood. It can lead to complete personality change, and in the most serious cases even to profound problems or suicide. Fortunately, schools are now much better prepared to deal with the problem than in the past. If you are concerned that your child is being bullied, you have a right to get the school to help you take practical steps to stop the bullies.

Spot the signs first of all – the earlier you respond, the more options you have. Key indicators include:

- Your child becomes very introverted or withdrawn.

- Their pocket money goes missing without reason.

- They pretend to be ill so they can stay at home or they start skipping school.

- They often have unexplained cuts or bruises.

- Their clothes are torn or damaged.

- They cannot account for the loss of a possession – like a computer game or watch.

- They become aggressive at home.

- Their schoolwork suffers.

- They seem anxious and have trouble sleeping.

If you know your child is being bullied, speak to them first and ask what they want to happen. Reassure them that they are not to blame and that whatever's happened can be fixed. Suggest some alternatives to your child – these could range from you contacting the school (an option they will probably hate in the first instance) to speaking informally to a teacher or classroom assistant.

How to . . . contact the school

1. Arrange a meeting with your child's class teacher and discuss your concerns in an open and positive manner – remember: you're looking for a solution, not for someone to blame.

2. Find out if there are any changes to your child's normal social life at school – are they being excluded in the playground, do they seem withdrawn in the classroom?

3. Find out whether the school operates an anti-bullying policy – they should – and whether there are any initiatives that could help your child, such as a friendship bench.

4. If you feel it is necessary, you can then arrange a meeting with the head of year or head teacher to find out about the level of supervision in the playground. Arrange a follow-up meeting to check the progress of the problem.

Bullying dos and don'ts

Do:

- Talk the problems through frankly and openly with your child. Where possible, try to get their agreement before you take any action.

- Give your child some coaching and coping strategies for the next bullying session.

- Help your child boost their own confidence levels by taking up a sport or martial art.

- Keep a diary of any bulling incidents.

- Support your child's social life by allowing them to invite new friends round to play or for sleepovers.

- Encourage them to take up after school activities and widen their horizons beyond school.

Don't:

- Storm into the school demanding justice for your little one.

- Assume the school knows that the bullying is taking place.

- Ignore the bullying – it is not character-building, and it can be quite the opposite. Take your child's fears seriously.

- Let your child stay at home to avoid the bullies. That won't help anyone and could lead to you being prosecuted and fined.

- Assume the school is your only hope. If you're not satisfied with their response, get in touch with the Local Education Authority (part of the county council) and speak to the education welfare officer.

What to do if . . . your child is a bully

Discovering that your own child is the bully can be just as trau-
matic as finding out they are being bullied. If you are told that
your child is bullying other children, don't get angry. Try the following instead:

● Tell your child what you know and ask for their side of the
story.

● Try to find out from the teacher whether any other children
were involved and whether there was a 'ringleader'.

● Ask your child to put themselves in the position of the
victim – how would they feel if this were happing to them?

● Ask the school to increase supervision at break times – and to
keep you informed if the bullying goes on.

● Find out if the bullying is the result of your child being bullied
themselves.

6

ESSENTIAL GENERAL KNOWLEDGE

The fundamental defect with fathers is that they want their children to be a credit to them.
Bertrand Russell

As we go through life we forget so much of the stuff we were taught at school. Then when our own children are going through the same learning process it's pretty humbling to realise you don't have a clue which king was which or who invented what and when. Here's your essential guide to all the basic theories, dates and names from history you'll need to impress your kids with.

🚗 HISTORY 🚗

KINGS AND QUEENS OF BRITAIN (FROM 1066)

1066 – William the First (AKA The Conqueror)
1087 – William II
1100 – Henry I
1135 – Stephen
1154 – Henry II
1189 – Richard I
1199 – John
1216 – Henry III

1272 – Edward I
1307 – Edward II
1327 – Edward III
1377 – Richard II
1399 – Henry IV
1413 – Henry V
1422 – Henry VI
1461 – Edward IV
1483 – Edward V
1483 – Richard III

1485 – Henry VII
1509 – Henry VIII
1547 – Edward VI
1553 – Mary I
1558 – Elizabeth I
1603 – James I (of England, VI of Scotland)
1625 – Charles I (beheaded)

1649 – Commonwealth (with Oliver Cromwell ruling as Lord Protector)

1660 – Charles II

1685 – James II

1689 – William III and Mary II

1702 – Anne

1714 – George I

1727 – George II

1760 – George III

1820 – George IV

1830 – William IV

1837 – Victoria

1901 – Edward VII

1910 – George V

1936 – Edward VIII (abdicated)

1936 – George VI

1952 – Elizabeth II

Pocket fact

Queen Victoria is currently the longest-serving British monarch in history, having ruled for 64 years.

KEY DATES IN BRITISH HISTORY

1,000,000 BC – *Homo erectus* makes fire

40,000 BC – Modern humans emerge in Europe

2500 BC – Pyramids built in Egypt; Stonehenge in UK

510 BC – Roman republic founded

43 AD – Roman armies conquer Britain

476 AD – Roman empire collapses

787 AD – Vikings invade Britain

1066 – Normans conquer Britain

1215 – Magna Carta signed at Runnymede

1348 – Black Death kills millions across UK and Europe

1475 – First book printed in English

1534 – Henry VIII establishes Church of England

1588 – Spanish Armada defeated

1605 – Gunpowder Plot fails to kill King James and Parliament

1649 – King Charles I beheaded

1653 – Oliver Cromwell becomes Lord Protector

1665 – Great Plague

1666 – Great Fire of London

1765 – James Hargreaves invents Spinning Jenny; Industrial Revolution begins

1776 – America declares independence

1800 – Act of Union between Britain and Ireland

1912 – *Titanic* sinks

1914-18 – First World War

1939-45 – Second World War

1989-90 – End of the Cold War

Pocket fact

There are 1,792 steps to the top of the Eiffel Tower in Paris. The French Revolution was completed in 1792. Coincidence? Probably not.

ROMAN NUMERALS

Latin may be a dead language, but its influence on our culture is still very strongly felt. Roman numerals are found everywhere, from the closing credits of TV shows to architecture all around us – even to the Superbowl. So what do the numerals mean and how do they work?

The basic numerals and their values are:

I = 1; V = 5; X = 10; L = 50; C = 100; D = 500; M = 1000

In general, the largest number comes first, followed by the smaller numbers down to one – so the number 18 would be expressed as XVIII (10+5+1+1+1). The year 2009 is a bit more complex because four and nine are expressed as IV and IX – ie one before five and one before 10. So 2009 would be MMIX (1000+1000+(1 less than 10 = 9)). 2010, however, is a lot simpler: MMX (1000+1000+10)

Latin is everywhere in our language – not just in the numerals but in everyday general use. There's an example above: 'ie' means 'id est' or 'that is', while eg means 'exempli gratia' (for example) and etc means 'et cetera' or 'and so on'.

🚗 SCIENCE 🚗

HUMAN EVOLUTION

Whether you choose to believe the works of Charles Darwin or you follow a creationist approach, there's pretty strong scientific evidence for the evolution of humans through the ages. Here's a quick rundown of the main ages that have led to the current fine example that you represent:

- *Australopithecus* – first evidence found is from approximately 4 million years BC, in Africa
- *Homo habilis* – first evidence approx. 2 million years BC, Africa
- *Homo erectus* – first evidence approximately 1.5 million years BC, Africa and Asia
- *Homo sapiens* – first evidence 400,000 BC, Africa, Asia and Europe
- **Neanderthal man** – first evidence 150,000 BC, Europe and Asia
- **Modern** *Homo sapiens* – first evidence 130,000 BC, Africa and Asia

Pocket fact
There is evidence that more than 500 species of animals have died out.

How to . . . become a Jurassic explorer

Living in a country with so much shoreline has its advantages, especially when you want to understand what the world was like millions of years before we were born. Fossils are created when sea creatures die and become encased in the silt and mud of the sea bed, which hardens over many years into rock.

Common fossils that can be found around Britain include:

- **Ammonite**. A type of sea snail that lived more than 60 million years ago.

- **Trilobite**. Similar in shape and appearance to a woodlouse, these are also sea creatures found in plentiful supply.

- **Fish and other sea creatures**. If you're really lucky you can find a fossilised fish skeleton – even some dinosaur fossils have been discovered down the years on the shoreline of England.

These fossils allow us to see for ourselves the bone structure and shape of these long-extinct creatures. Usually the fossils are encased in rock, which is why fossil hunters need a flat bladed hammer to split rocks and get at the bounty inside. You can find a plentiful supply of fossils in the following places:

- Dorset coast – particularly around Lyme Regis
- East Yorkshire coast – Whitby and surrounding area
- Cumbria coast

THE SUN AND THE STARS

Astronomy is a fascinating science, made all the more incredible by our endless fascination with gazing into the night sky. One day we'll visit every planet in our solar system, but until then you'll have to make do with this quick guide (from the middle outwards):

The Sun
Surface temperature: 6,000°C
Facts: The daddy. No matter how important Simon Cowell thinks he is, the sun is boss of the solar system and all life depends on its continuing existence. But don't worry, it's been around for about five billion years and is expected to survive for around the same time into the future. We all revolve around it.

Mercury
Surface temperature: 400°C
Facts: Named after the messenger to the Roman gods, because its progress around the sun is so much quicker than any other planet – there are just under 88 days in a Mercury year.

Venus
Surface temperature: 480°C
Facts: The brightest planet in the sky, which makes it the easiest to observe from Earth. Venus is named after the Roman goddess of love. And why not – she's very pretty.

Earth
Surface temperature: ranges from –80°C to 55°C approx
Facts: Our home, and the only planet in the solar system that has the capacity to support us naturally. Which is lucky. The planet's core is liquid.

Mars
Surface temperature: –50°C approx
Facts: Mars is named after the Roman god of war, and with pretty good reason. It is a hostile looking place with severe dust storms.

Pocket fact 🔑

Pluto was discovered in 1930 and was upgraded to 'major' planet status. However it was downgraded again in 2007.

Jupiter
Surface temperature: –160°C approx
Facts: This planet has around 60 moons, some of which can be seen through an ordinary telescope. It is named after Zeus, the chief Roman god.

Saturn
Surface temperature: up to –190°C
Facts: Saturn is famous for its rings – a collection of rock that floats in orbit around the planet. It takes nearly 30 of our years for Saturn to pass around the sun. It is named after Zeus' father.

Uranus
Surface temperature: up to −220°C
Facts: While we don't know much about Uranus, we do know that it takes 87 years to circle the sun. Uranus was Zeus' grandfather.

Neptune
Surface temperature: unknown, but really, really cold
Facts: Named after the god of the sea and pretty much composed of ice around rock, it's a relatively unknown quantity – although a space probe, the Voyager 2, did reach the surface in the 1980s.

Pocket fact 🏌

The UK is approximately 244,756sq km, making it 37.5 times smaller than the USA (at 9,160,460sq km). The UK's population is around 60 million, a mere 4.5 times smaller than the USA's 275 million.

🚗 MATHS 🚗

USEFUL SUMS AND FORMULAE

How to figure out a percentage
Find 1% by dividing whole by 100 (eg 31 ÷ 100 = 0.31). Then multiply that number by the percentage amount you want to find (eg 6% would be 0.31 × 6 = 1.86. So 6% of 31 is 1.86).

Percentages as fractions:

$$10\% = 1/10$$
$$20\% = 1/5$$
$$25\% = 1/4$$
$$50\% = 1/2$$
$$75\% = 3/4$$

Decimals
Numbers to the left of a decimal point are whole numbers. Numbers to the right are decimal fractions.

Prime numbers

A prime number is a number that can only be divided by itself and 1.

The first 26 prime numbers are 2, 3, 5, 7, 11, 13, 17, 19, 23, 29, 31, 37, 41, 43, 47, 53, 59, 61, 67, 71, 73, 79, 83, 89, 97, 101.

Some useful equations

Area: length × width = number of square units

Area of a circle: $\pi \times$ radius^2 (where $\pi = 3.14$)

Perimeter: add all lengths together

Volume: length × width × height = number of cubic units

Circumference of a circle: $2\pi r$ ($2 \times \pi \times$ radius)

Area of a triangle: $1/2 \times$ length × height

Speed: distance ÷ time

Time: distance ÷ speed

Distance: speed × time

How to . . . know everything (the long and the short of it)

Just in case your children (or grandchildren) ever ask, here's a concise breakdown of the key facts of our world:

- The world's largest island is Greenland
- The world's largest country is Russia
- The world's smallest country is the Vatican City
- The world's largest ocean is the Pacific
- The world's largest lake is the Caspian Sea
- The world's longest river is the Nile
- The world's highest mountain is Mount Everest
- The world's largest continent is Asia
- The world's flattest continent is Oceania
- The world's highest waterfall is the Angel Falls in Venezuela
- The highest temperature ever recorded was 58°C (in Libya)

- The lowest temperature ever recorded was −89°C (in Antarctica)

Pocket fact 🏌

Burj Khalifa in Dubai, the world's tallest building at over 800m (2,625ft), also holds the record for the most storeys, highest observation platform and tallest service elevator. It's not only the tallest building in the world but also the tallest man-made structure.

7

NATIONAL BANK OF DAD: MONEY

A father carries pictures where his money used to be.
Unknown

The cost of having children is enormous. A survey has revealed that it can cost almost £194,000 to raise a child from birth to the age of 21. That's roughly £25 a day for 21 years. Childcare and education are the biggest costs facing parents and the expenses rise from around £9,000 in their first year to almost £14,000 once they reach 18. You need to be prepared for your child's future and you also need to negotiate those delicate issues such as pocket money. This chapter will give you the advice you need before you start panicking at the thought of all those pound signs flashing by.

🚗 YOUR CHILD'S MONEY 🚗

SAVING FOR YOUR CHILD

There are many ways to save for your children's future. Some accounts are dedicated to the child – and are not usually accessible until they are 18 – while other methods allow you to save for specific goals with easier access to the funds. Here's a guide to some of the most common methods on the market.

Child Trust Funds

These were introduced back in 2002, and all children receive a minimum of a £250 investment voucher from the government at birth. They receive another voucher at the age of seven. Children of lower income families receive up to £500. The money must be placed in a special fund – there are many on the market, of varying quality. You can invest a further £1,200 per year into the fund, which can be composed of a straight savings account or a higher-return (but riskier) investment account. Check out price comparison websites such as www.moneysupermarket.com to find out the best deals available, but beware of the admin fees on these funds – they can often eat up a large chunk of the interest.

ISAs

The Individual Savings Account is a good way to build up some cash reserves for major life events – such as buying a car or funding a holiday. The money saved in the account is free of UK income tax and can be saved in a combination of cash ISAs and investment ISAs, although there is an upper limit on the amount you can save in any tax year – this varies depending on your individual circumstances. Check the HMRC website (www.hmrc.gov.uk) or contact your bank for details of what is available to you.

National Savings and Investments

This is a government-backed scheme which offers a really good rate of interest for child savers, and lower than average risk. The interest on your child's savings is also tax free.

Top five non-traditional investments

1. **Fine art and books**. *If you've got any insider knowledge then you should buy up the works of an up-and-coming artist or author – first editions and original works/ etchings can be worth a fortune down the line.*
2. **Fine wine**. *Wine is a long-term investment. Either buy a sure-thing investment from the stocks of a well-known French vineyard, or get in on the ground floor by investing in a New World vineyard.*
3. **Property**. *With the current fluctuating market, property is due for a slow growth period over the next five to 10 years. An investment now could reach its peak when it's needed for university fees.*

4. ***Toys and games***. *Boxed, mint-condition toys are one of the best investments in terms of the return you'd expect a few years down the line. Limited production runs or cult action figures are always a good buy.*
5. ***Shares in a start-up***. *A pretty risky way to invest, but if you can bankroll research into a new technology or choose the right start-up, you might just ride the crest of an investment wave.*

POCKET MONEY

The amount of pocket money you should give and the basis on which it's given are fairly personal choices, but how can you know what's 'normal' and what's miserly when you're setting an amount of pocket money?

Pocket fact

A national survey of pocket money was carried out by the Halifax in July 2008. It discovered that the average weekly pocket money was £6.13 per week (down from £8.01 the previous year). However, the survey does also explain that mobiles, clothes, transport and big ticket electrical items are often excluded from the pocket money calculation.

How much to give?

You need to consider what you want the pocket money to do – is it a catch-all expenses payment that covers phone and travel costs as well as going out, buying food, music and clothes? Make a list of what you expect your child to buy with it, and work out how much this would cost per week.

What pocket money might be for:
- Transport costs
- Sweets and snacks

- Magazines and books
- Toys
- Clothes other than school uniform
- Christmas and birthday presents for other people
- Mobile phone credit
- Going out costs, such as cinema and concert tickets
- School supplies, such as stationery
- Toiletries and make-up

Teaching responsibility

Some parents feel that pocket money provides a good opportunity to learn the value of money. They link the amount of money given directly to chores the child does around the house – like a performance-related pay. It's a theory that works, but only if it is enforced – you've got to be strong enough to follow through on a threat of cutting off funds if they don't play ball. And most people aren't.

A third way

A compromise between giving children everything they want and making them work for every penny is to provide funds for the basics while encouraging them to save a portion of their pocket money for the big ticket item they want. This works really well if you're prepared to match-fund the item. Say, for example, Johnny wants a computer game costing £40 and he puts aside £2 a week for 10 weeks, you'll split the cost of the game with him. This approach makes saving accessible and builds good practice.

'When I was a lad' . . . *money was worth the following*

- *£15 pocket money today is worth the equivalent of £1 in 1960.*
- *£10 pocket money today is worth the equivalent of £1 in 1970.*

- *£5 pocket money today is worth the equivalent of £1 in 1975.*
- *£3 pocket money today is worth the equivalent of £1 in 1980.*
- *£1.50 pocket money today is worth the equivalent of £1 in 1990.*

Other ways to encourage saving

- **Building interest**. As well as rewards for chores and the 'matched funding' idea outlined above, you can encourage children to save by opening a savings account for them. Most give good rates of interest for long term savings. The process of opening and managing the account is a great way to help your child feel as if they are contributing to their own financial future.

- **Monthly bonus**. Switching your teen's allowance to a monthly direct debit will help them to feel more independent and will teach them the value of budgeting long before they move out and have to juggle their own finances.

What you need to agree with your child

- Can pocket money be supplemented by doing extra chores around the house?

- When is it due for review? Is there an automatic raise every birthday?

- Is part of it earmarked for savings? What happens to additional money such as for birthday gifts?

- Are they allowed to borrow in advance? What is the limit on this?

- Can it be withheld as punishment for bad behaviour?

- Is there anything they can't buy with their pocket money? (Eg you may wish to stop young children from spending it all on sweets.)

🚗 YOUR ADULT CHILD'S MONEY 🚗

It's a myth to assume that once your children have left home they'll be financially independent. In fact, they'll probably cost you more once they've gone than they ever did under your roof. This is especially true for the university years.

STUDENTS

A university education provides many great benefits, but it also brings a fair degree of debt to the unwary. You can help your child at university with the following tips:

- **Banking**. Make sure your child chooses the best student bank account – a comparison of the alternatives will show you which offer cash back or other bonuses, such as free railcards for new customers.

- **Loans**. The student loan is still the best way to pay your way though university – you won't find a better financial package for your child unless you're paying the tuition fees yourself. If any top-up loans are needed, you might consider taking these out under your own name – you'll almost certainly get a better rate of interest and it will work out cheaper in the long run than a credit card.

- **Fringe benefits**. Don't forget that there are many other financial benefits to being a student. Many shops offer discounts on the production of an NUS card. Train and bus services also offer heavily subsidised deals for students.

Pocket fact 🔔
The average student leaves university with £23,000 of debt.

ADULTS

The most likely financial disaster your adult offspring will present you with is a crippling debt caused by too much spending and not enough earning. This can often come about when they are newly independent and living a single life. It may be the first time they've ever managed a household budget and things can get pretty complicated. You can help them in a couple of different ways:

- **Plan of action**. Sit them down and work out what they earn and what they owe. Focus on high-interest loans and credit card debt, getting them to place all the debt onto a zero per cent card (some of these offer up to a year's interest free loan) while they organise their finances.

- **Help, but only as a last resort**. Paying off the debt of your adult offspring is only wise if they genuinely have no other reasonable option. Their best bet is to dig themselves out of the hole they've made, but with your support.

The top five richest people in the world

1. **Bill Gates** – *Founder of Microsoft*
2. **Warren Buffet** – *US investment guru*
3. **Carlos Slim Helu** – *Mexican communications magnate*
4. **Lawrence Ellison** – *Founder of Oracle*
5. **Ingvar Kamprad** – *Founder of IKEA*

How to . . . write a will

As a family man, it's essential you have a will in place so that your wishes are honoured in the event of your death. Many people opt to have a solicitor draw up their will so that it has a secure legal footing, but you can do it yourself.

All you need to make a will legally binding are the following:

1. **Be an adult**. Only persons of 18 years and over can make a will.

2. **Be of 'sound mind'**. You can't make a will if you aren't aware of the process and of the implications of your choices. You must never be forced or persuaded into making a will.

3. **Write it**. A legal will must be written down.

4. **Sign it**. You need to add your signature to the will in the presence of two witnesses. The witnesses – who must not be beneficiaries of the will (or be married to beneficiaries of the will) must also sign it.

The content of the will isn't just limited to your financial arrangements: it should also include details of your funeral wishes; your nominated guardians in the event that both you and your partner die; and the executors of the will – two trusted people who will ensure that your wishes are carried out.

As a general guideline, if your financial arrangements are complex – with lots of property, investments or a business to pass on – then you should get legal help when making your will. If your family arrangements are complex – divorces, step-children or remarriages – it's also a good idea to organise legal assistance.

Otherwise, simply make sure you've recorded all your assets, explained clearly who they are going to and follow the steps above to make it all legal. And don't forget to keep it somewhere safe but easily accessible – remember that you want it to be found when you aren't around.

Pocket tip 🍺

Remember to revisit your will after any major life event – a death, a marriage, a birth or a divorce could all affect the details of a will.

🚗 **WORKING WITH A YOUNG FAMILY** 🚗

It's easy to resign yourself to the fact that as a working father you'll never see much of your kids in the week and you'll be pretty tired when you do see them at weekends. But there are things you can do to increase your time with your children. Here, we give you a few ideas:

- **Start early**. Starting work an hour earlier in the morning and finishing earlier at night might be the difference between reading a bedtime story and getting home after they're asleep – and it shouldn't make any difference to your employer. You could even do things the other way around – have a routine that involves you making breakfast for the kids and doing the school run before the working day starts.

- **'Ring-fence' some time**. If you do find yourself working long hours, try to find at least one day a week when you can get home early enough to take over the bedtime routine of baths and stories. It'll give your kids something memorable to look forward to.

- **Maximise the weekends**. We all know that work is a necessary part of life, but try not to allow it to creep into your weekend. Your boss doesn't have the right to take up your out-of-hours time and your downtime with the family is essential for your own well-being. So make sure you are actually spending the weekend together as a family: don't spend your Sundays playing golf or ferrying your kids around the shops unless these things are really important. Instead, do something planned as a group – like visiting a theme park or having a meal out.

- **Flexible working**. Many companies will consider a reasonable request for flexible hours, especially if it comes with a benefit for them. Simply saying, 'I need to spend more time with my children' won't do it, nor will, 'I can fit my job into four days easily'. Instead, work out a scheme that allows you to work afternoons at home, for example, which gives you post-school time with the kids and then a longer working day into early evening.

🚗 WORKING FOR YOURSELF 🚗

While running your own business sounds like a great lifestyle choice (time off when you want; able to help around the house), the reality can be very different. If you're the breadwinner, everything rests on your shoulders – you alone have to ensure the money keeps coming in. It can also be really hard to take holidays when you're self-employed as the downside to flexible working is that your customers expect you to be on hand all the time.

Top ten famous older fathers

1. **Saul Bellow** – author (became a father at 84)
2. **Charlie Chaplin** – film star (73)
3. **Des O'Connor** – entertainer (72)
4. **Pierre Trudeau** – Canadian politician (72)
5. **Pablo Picasso** – painter (68)
6. **Luciano Pavarotti** – singer (67)
7. **Warren Beatty** – actor (62)
8. **David Jason** – actor (61)
9. **Paul McCartney** – musician (61)
10. **Rod Stewart** – musician (60)

I've got three kids and no money – why can't I have no kids and three money?
Homer J Simpson

DAD AND YOUR LAD

By the time a man realises that maybe his father was right, he usually has a son who thinks he's wrong.
Charles Wadsworth

🚗 BONDING WITH YOUR BOY 🚗

Whatever is said about the changing role of fathers in the family, one thing is true: your role as a dad includes giving your son support, encouragement and praise. Boys need a lot of 'well done son' support and your bonding time with him gives you a whole range of opportunities to give those emotional pats on the back that will encourage him to explore the world with greater confidence.

Top five ultimate British sporting heroes:

1. **Sir Ian Botham**. *Took on the might of the Australians at cricket and tackled his personal demons at the same time – and won.*
2. **Sir Steven Redgrave**. *The ultimate Olympian, Steve Redgrave's fistful of gold medals is unlikely to be equalled by any British athlete.*
3. **Sir Denis Compton** *Represented his country at both football and cricket, and he had immaculate hair. What a guy.*
4. **Sir Stirling Moss** *A great driver from the days when you had to be great to be a driver.*
5. **Sir Geoff Hurst** *Scorer of the most famous hat-trick in English football.*

TAKE HIM TO A FOOTBALL MATCH

The first trip to a football match is a rite of passage that involves some careful planning and consideration.

You'll win nothing with youngsters

Judging whether your child is of an appropriate age to stand up to the rigours of a football match is a pretty tricky call. It's totally subjective, but as a rule you should wait until they're seven or above, just because the attention span and stamina required to sit for the best part of two hours in a cold stadium is beyond most small kids. The first match should be preceded by a few TV games, a lot of discussion of what you'll see and maybe even a stadium tour (not necessarily on a match day) so that your boy can get a good feel for the experience before he's launched into it.

Any more of that and you're off

When you do take the plunge and go to a game, be aware that the language from fellow supporters will be appalling – even if you've got seats in the family enclosure. Exposure to swearing doesn't necessarily mean you'll end up with a boy who curses like a navvy, but you may get some awkward, 'Dad, what does xxxx mean?' questions in the car.

Blue or red, it's not black and white

You're fighting a losing battle if you want to force your boy to follow your team. Positive reinforcement of an early interest might help you – along with a few visits to the club shop – but in truth, if you're a die-hard Woking fan you may struggle to have your lad resist the siren-like pull of the Premier League big guns. It's just a fad.

Join the club

If your boy does fall for a team in a big way, most have junior supporters' clubs that allow kids to get discounts on tickets and merchandise, as well as access to a range of exclusive club events.

Pocket fact 🏌

*The average footballer covers around seven miles per game –
although most of this is spent chasing after the referee.*

GO FISHING

The great advantage of fishing is that it fulfils most of the key cri-
teria of dad and lad bonding time. Namely:

● It's cheap
● It's a good way to spend a few hours together
● There's something to do when you can't think of anything to say
● Anyone can master the basics

Of course, like all sports and pastimes, you can find plenty of ways
to spend your money, but in essence all you'll need is a couple of
cheap rods and a few accessories. You'll also need a licence to fish
(obtainable from the Environment Agency), as well as permission
to go on any land that isn't public. Your lad (if he is under 12)
doesn't need a licence.

Make sure you take plenty to eat and drink – including hot drinks.
Wrap up well, even on a fairly warm day, as you'll be stationary
for the most part of the day. And don't forget to take something
to sit on.

Pocket fact 🏌

*Close season for river fishing: March to June each year
Close season for fish: Salmon – 1 November to 31 January;
Trout – 1 October to end February*

GO ON A WEEKEND CAMPING TRIP

Camping is a little like fishing in that it is a cheap and focused way
to spend your time together. The weather conditions will determine

the amount of kit you require but as a minimum you should be looking to take:

- Tent (obviously!)
- Groundsheet
- Mattresses
- Sleeping bags
- Stove
- Lighter
- Plates and cutlery
- First aid kit
- Mobile phone
- Torches

Just about everything else is optional. Take plenty of clothes that can build up in layers so that you can discard a layer if it gets wet. Don't be tempted to set up camp in the wilds of a forest – go for a licensed site as there will be facilities that you'll be glad of in the middle of the night.

Before you go for a proper camping trip, you could try an overnight stay in the garden. Use all the kit, and avoid skipping back into the house to get midnight snacks or another jumper. The purpose of the trial run is to see how you both cope with life under canvas.

What to eat

Don't overwhelm yourself with a complex menu. Take stuff that you can keep dry if it is wet, won't go off if it's hot and can be cooked easily. Bacon and beans are a camping favourite, along with simple snack foods like crackers, pâtés, dried fruit and some raw vegetables with dips. To heat food, take along a simple gas ring.

What to do

A proper camping trip needs proper activities – essentials include a ghostly story, some songs, some jokes and a game of cards.

- Even if you're camping in the height of summer it'll be dark after 10pm, so don't do anything that needs lots of light.

- Take a book of ghost stories, like those of Edgar Allen Poe or Washington Irving.

- Make up your own story to tell in a 'round' with one sentence each.

- If you do have your own small fire (these may be banned on some sites), make sure it is well ringed by stones to stop it getting out of control and don't use any artificial accelerants to get it going. Don't forget the marshmallows and some water-soaked skewers to cook them on.

BE HIS SIDELINE SUPPORTER

If your boy is a sports fanatic then when he's not watching sport, he's most likely playing it. You have a part to play here too, but it must be well judged or you could end up taking over or coming across as too pushy. Follow these basic steps:

- **Keep perspective**. This is something your son is doing that you are following. Don't try to lead him in a direction because you think it is best, don't criticise him (or any of his team mates for that matter), and don't forget that this is a bonding exercise. He's looking for your love, support and praise – not your man-management skills.

- **Keep under control**. Pride in your son's achievements is great, but don't let your support boil over into abuse of officials, coaches or other parents. One part of the essential skills your son is learning from sport is respect for authority. He'll be looking to you as a role model, so don't let him down.

- **Don't quit: commit**. Remember that you're likely to be doing a lot of driving around, picking up and dropping off – there will be matches to watch, equipment to buy and maintain and a training routine to adhere to. This is a commitment for you both and by honouring it happily yourself you can ensure he will do likewise.

PLAY CRICKET

Most boys have football down to a T. Cricket still suffers from an image problem, based on the myth that it requires a surface of perfectly manicured grass and a stack of cash to buy all the kit. In fact, all you need for a game of cricket is a half-decent bat, a ball of some sort and a target to aim at (chalk stumps on a brick wall are perfectly acceptable).

Pocket tip 🍺

If you want to get your child interested in the sport, first of all go to a 20-20 game. This is a shortened form of one-day cricket, often played over the course of a summer's evening, and it has all the razzmatazz of football, with lots of noise, big-hitting and excitement. Compared to the drizzly second day of a division two championship match limping towards a draw, it's much more of a spectacle for the young fan.

Cricket – the basics

1. **Wicket**. This is the name of the set of three vertical wooden **stumps** topped by two horizontal **bails** at either end of the 22 yard (about 20m) playing pitch. In longer forms of the game (more than one day) each team bats for two **innings**.

2. **Crease**. The batsman stands in a chalk-marked area known as a **crease**. This area is like a 'base', in which he is safe from being run out or stumped.

3. **Over**. The bowler bowls a set of six consecutive balls, known as an **over** (some forms of the game have eight ball overs).

4. **Fielding positions**. The names of fielding positions are notoriously difficult. Without going into great detail, the most important things to remember are that the fielders to the right of a right handed batsman are on the 'off' side (mid off, long off) and those to the left are on the 'leg' or 'on' side (mid on, long on, square leg etc). If a fielding position is

prefixed with 'silly' (silly point, for example) it tells you that the fielder is close to the bat, which can be a pretty silly place to be.

5. **Scoring**. Batsmen can score six (by hitting the ball out of the field of play without it hitting the ground), four (out of the field, but hitting the ground first) or an unlimited combination of runs (but in practice rarely more than three) by running between the wickets. Runs are also scored from **wides** (when the ball is bowled so wide that the batsman can't realistically play a shot), **no balls** (when the bowler releases the ball with his front foot outside of the crease), **byes** (when the ball misses the bat, wicket and wicketkeeper), and **leg byes** (when the ball hits the batsman's leg and runs away).

6. **Batting**. The aim of batting is essentially to score runs and preserve your wicket. Orthodox scoring shots are **drives**, **pulls**, **hooks**, **cuts**, **sweeps**, and **glances**, and defence is either by placing one foot forward (known as **front-foot defence**) or by standing back in front of the wicket (**back-foot defence**). The choice of shot depends on the length and direction of the ball bowled.

7. **Bowling**. Bowling is generally categorised in three ways: **fast**, **swing**, and **spin**. Fast bowling is all about the pace of the bowler's run-up, delivery and follow-through. A smooth bowling action is essential. Swing bowling depends more on the condition of the ball. For the ball to swing, one side of the ball's surface should be shinier than the other, meaning it will curve as it flies through the air. This is why the ball is rubbed frantically on trousers between overs. Spin bowling uses a combination of the seam that runs down the middle of the ball and a twist of the bowler's hand to make the ball move after it has pitched.

8. **Results**. Longer forms of cricket – test matches and county championship games – can finish in a draw if all four innings haven't been completed or if the team batting fourth hasn't

reached the total set by their opponents. Shorter (limited overs) games cannot be drawn: they can only be tied if the two teams' scores are level at the end of the match. If a limited overs game is shortened by the weather, a revised total is calculated using an adjusted score worked out using the Duckworth-Lewis (D/L) method.

Cricket World Cup winners

1975 – West Indies	**1996** – Sri Lanka
1979 – West Indies	**1999** – Australia
1983 – India	**2003** – Australia
1987 – Australia	**2007** – Australia
1992 – Pakistan	

England have been in the Cricket World Cup Final three times but have never won.

Cricket terminology – ways to get out (or not to!)

- **LBW (leg before wicket)**. If a ball is bowled in such a way that it hits (or would hit) the ground in line with the wickets and would then go on to hit the wicket, but strikes the bats-man on the leg instead, the umpire may decide the ball would have hit the wicket and will give him out.

- **Stumped**. If the batsman moves his body and bat outside the popping crease when attempting to play a shot and misses the ball, the wicketkeeper can break the wicket with the ball.

- **Hit wicket**. If the batsman steps backwards and breaks the wicket while attempting to play a shot he is given out. As in all the above cases, the wicket is awarded to the bowler.

- **Run out**. If batsmen are attempting a run and the ball is thrown to either wicket and they cannot get their bat or any part of their body into the popping crease first, they can be run out by a member of the fielding side.

- **Handled ball**. If a batsman deliberately handles the ball to stop it hitting the wicket, he is out.

- **Hit ball twice**. If a batsman deliberately hits any delivery twice, he is given out.

- **Obstructing a fielder**. If a batsman stands in the way of any member of the fielding side, he can be given out by the umpire.

🚗 WORKING TOGETHER 🚗

Top ten things for dads to do with their sons

Boy time is vital – you and your son need to build up a strong bond now to get you through the hard times when he's a sullen teenager and you're a stressed executive. Making time for each other requires some thought and planning: use the following as examples of what you can achieve together.

1. **Woodwork**. Fretwork, as it used to be known, is the act of making small-scale wooden items using a minimal toolkit. A fret saw, hammer, nails and the kind of ready-sawn accessory kits you can get from craft shops will get you started on model cars, wooden animals and boats – moving on up to more ambitious projects such as a knight's castle over time.

2. **Build a go-kart**. If you get the crafting habit, you could try knocking up a simple go-kart together. The best kind of cart uses pram wheels – you can often pick these up at boot fairs or from charity shops. Fix the wheels to the ends of strong wooden axles and then brace these onto a strong body. Depending on the level of complexity of the kart – and on your creative skills – you can add steering and braking mechanisms that will make the kart really state-of-the-art.

3. **Make a model**. For the less technically competent dad who still wants the pleasure of creating something with his boy, model kits are a marvel. Although these kits are a bit fiddly for little hands, from seven years upwards your boy will be

able to tackle a simple kit without problems. Get two kits, so you can work together in parallel.

4. **Make a train set**. An extension of the modelling idea, but much broader and easier to do as a collaboration.

   • Get hold of a simple oval electric train set and, rather than paying a fortune for ready-made accessories, build your own tunnels, hills, roads and houses.

   • Start with a thick piece of chipboard and build up the landscape using papier-mâché.

   • Use metal garden mesh for the tunnels, again coated in papier-mâché.

   • The houses can be made from cardboard, or you can sometimes buy pre-decorated flat pack card models from hobby shops.

5. **Make paper aeroplanes**. You can use up a precious hour with paper aeroplanes, especially if it's nice enough to fly them outside. The construction of the plane is a matter of personal choice, but generally the best planes are those where the top corners are folded once into the centre, smoothed down, and folded again, making an A4 sheet into almost a triangle. Form the wings from this shape, so that the plane looks like a Concorde aeroplane. Keep the body to a minimum and the wingspan to a maximum. Putting a small paper clip on the nose sometimes helps with balance. Make a few planes, get your boy to decorate them, and get racing.

6. **Build a swing**. If you're lucky enough to have a decent load-bearing tree in your garden with a horizontal branch, then that tree deserves its own swing. A basic swing is easy to knock up.

   • Take a smooth, strong piece of wood and drill four holes in it, each about 5cm from a corner.

   • Now take two pieces of rope of equal length and knot them through two of the holes, throw the rope over the branch, adjust the seat to the right height (so that your boy can get his feet flat on the ground while on the seat if needed) and then tie off the other ends of the ropes.

7. **Make a den**. Dens are mysterious places, often built from dubious materials like sheets, driftwood, pallets, and anything else that happens to be lying around. But that is their magic. The most important feature of a den is that it must be hidden from general sight. There should be just enough room for the two of you, some snacks and a torch. It's the prefect place to tell ghost stories.

8. **Put on a show of jokes and tricks**. Magic tricks are great for kids. Firstly they are amazed by them and then they want to how it's done so they can impress everyone else. You can get hold of card tricks and illusions that you can practise together, or turn to page 108 for some other ideas.

9. **Go for a 'survival' ramble**. Much more than a walk, a manly 'survival' ramble will make you feel like Bear Grylls and Ray Mears at once. What you need is a good solid stick for slashing undergrowth, a bag to collect natural foods (hedgerow fruits good; mushrooms bad) and a spirit of adventure. Go off the beaten track, but make sure you do it with plenty of daylight available and a mobile phone in your pocket. Otherwise, go nuts, wild man.

10. **Weird (and wonderful) science**. Science is more than just a school subject. It's an opportunity to explore the natural and physical world in a whole range of fun experiments. See page 111 for how to do these experiments . . .

9

DADDY'S GIRL

*A father is always making his baby into a little woman. And when she is
a woman he turns her back again.*
Enid Bagnold

🚗 GETTING ON WITH YOUR GIRL 🚗

A father is the most important man in his girl's life for anything
up to the first 20 years of her life – and sometimes well beyond
that. He's the yardstick against which she will judge other men
against and his word is the law. No pressure, then.

The time you spend with your daughter is special – especially if
work keeps you apart for large periods of the week. So it's important to plan your time together well. Here are some good tips for
activities that suit a range of ages.

DADS AND TODDLERS

Nature walk and feeding the ducks

The simplest activities can also be the most rewarding. A bag of
stale bread and a duck pond provide the focus for some really
good bonding time. It's a good chance to practise language with a
toddler – talk about everything you see on the walk to the pond
and find out what she recalls on the way back.

Crafty make and do

Little girls tend to have a good capacity for sitting still and
focusing on one task at a time, which means craft activities are
excellent ways to spend time together. Get a range of craft
materials – a ream of cheap white paper or a pile of discarded

paperwork from the office are good starting points. Get a glue stick, some shiny paper, some glitter and felt and start creating. Once she's in the swing she'll churn things out at a frantic pace, so it can be useful to have a specific project in mind: 'Let's make mummy a card', rather than just slapping bits of paper together at random. Remember to dress her in something that can stand mess before you begin – and keep plenty of hand wipes nearby.

Dressing up box

Boys and girls both love dressing up, but there's something particularly special about a girl's dressing up box. It's the place where they first experiment with imaginative play. You can kit a dressing up box out cheaply with some rummaging around at jumble sales and in the bottom of your wardrobe. Speak to your own mother about old handbags and accessories (but make it clear why you're asking!). The more 'grown-up' the item, the more your girl will love it.

Music and dance

Whether you have aspirations of turning your daughter into a diva, or just want a way to use up some energy, you can foster a love of all things musical with a simple dance session. Get some classic dancing tunes – ABBA, Bee Gees or even the dreaded *High School Musical* – clear the furniture to the side of the room and do some simple dances. She'll love learning a bit of a routine. Don't worry about looking stupid – this is the one time in your life when your daughter will actually admire your dance moves.

DADS AND PRE-TEENS

Tom-boy time

Girls get pigeon-holed. That's a fact we can't deny and with so much gender-reinforcing advertising out there and so little time for parents to turn the tide, we can't really expect little girls to do anything other than love dolls, horses, puppies and pink. But your special time with your little girl can be different:

- **Practise a sport**. Golf, football, cricket and tennis are all games that you can practise one-to-one.

- **Teach her a skill**. Practical crafts like woodwork are a mystery to many girls. Working together on a simple project is a great way to bond.

- **Wild in the garden**. Give her a vegetable patch and help her to prepare it, sow seeds and maintain the plants.

- **Take her camping**. See page 93.

Top five ultimate British sporting heroines

1. ***Dame Ellen Macarthur***. *Round-the-world yachtswoman with more courage and fight than an entire premier league of male sports stars.*
2. ***Paula Radcliffe***. *She might have been plagued by injuries but Paula is a great example of sporting stamina. She has come back again and again, making her a great role model.*
3. ***Dame Kelly Holmes***. *Not just a great athlete, but a great ambassador for sport in general.*
4. ***Tanni Grey-Thompson***. *See above but times it by 10. She has forced Paralympic sport into the limelight and has helped it to be taken seriously.*
5. ***Virginia Wade***. *She won Wimbledon. That makes her the female Geoff Hurst, and it also proves that ability triumphs in the end.*

Get sporty

Sport is a great way to have a connection without complication, as you can focus on the day-to-day elements when necessary.

Help her make the right choice. There aren't many sports your daughter can't pursue, though in some areas she might find it difficult to locate a girls' rugby or cricket team. Think about her other interests — is there any way you can tie these together, like a love of animals with horse-riding, or a love of water with swimming or sailing.

Fix a budget and a timetable. Whichever sport she chooses you will need to make a joint commitment to it — that means buying kit, maintaining kit, attending practice sessions and/or matches. Make sure you can realistically afford the time and money to help her get as far as she can in her chosen sport.

Soccer dad?

One of the fastest-growing girls' sports around the world is football. If you're looking for something sporting to share you can't do much better.

- *Simplicity and accessibility. Football really can be played anywhere. Accessories are cheap and if you've got sports channels on your TV you can watch it 24/7.*
- *Good models. The sport is currently packed with positive role models in the shape of an exceptionally good national women's team. This isn't just good for the sport's profile, it's good for grass roots funding — with more girls' teams starting up than ever before.*
- *Fit and fast. Football improves coordination, stamina and team-working skills. In an age where we're all frantic about childhood obesity it's one of the safest and simplest ways to exercise.*

Make a puppet theatre

Extending the world of dressing up into drama is a natural progression of imagination. It's a limitless craft project — you need a good-sized box of at least 15 × 30cm (preferably a wooden box, but tough card will do), then you need to add curtains to the front and a backcloth. Make the puppets from card and attach them to lolly sticks. Start with some classic stories — Snow White, Cinderella or The Three Little Pigs — and just let your imaginations run wild. You can make scenery, change backcloths and curtains until you have a whole season of different shows.

Princess shopping

Your daughter will quite possibly want to take many of her 'rite of passage' steps in life with her mum. And, for that matter, your partner will probably want to be there for the first shoes, first party dress, first make-up and so on. Make your mark with the occasional VIP shopping trip, where you personally chauffeur her to a big department store, attend to her every need, buy something new and treat her to an ice cream afterwards. Even getting school shoes turns into something special with the right preparation.

DADS AND TEENAGERS

Lunch/dinner date

The success of this idea depends entirely on how it is pitched to your daughter. If she thinks she's going out with her dad to learn the social niceties of dating, she will run a mile. But if she just thinks you are taking her out for dinner so that you can have a chat and some quality time, she'll feel grown up and valued. *And* she'll learn the social niceties of dating. If you go somewhere nice, treat her kindly, open doors for her and make sure the conversation repeatedly comes around to topics that interest her, you will be setting her up for socialising – and helping her identify the characteristics to look for in a good partner.

Driving me crazy

Driving lessons can be stressful (see page 35 for more details) but they can also give a father and daughter a real focus for their time together. Remember that praise and reassurance breeds confidence and this in turn breeds responsibility. Even if you just have the occasional lesson to support her professional instruction, this is a great chance to show an interest in a vital life skill.

Let her lead

Teenage girls can be pretty headstrong, so trying to second-guess the things that she would like to do may lead to disaster. Instead, ask her outright if there's anything she'd like your help with, or just take the time to have a conversation on her terms (like on the dinner date outlined above). If you can talk to her and let her lead the conversation, you'll soon find things that interest her. Even if they don't interest you, they do provide a way into a more meaningful relationship.

Famous daddy's girls

- *Peaches and Pixie Geldof: daughters of Bob Geldof*
- *Lily Allen: daughter of Keith Allen*
- *Daisy Lowe: daughter of Gavin Rossdale*
- *Jaime Winstone: daughter of Ray Winstone*
- *Elisabeth Jagger: daughter of Mick Jagger*
- *Liv Tyler: daughter of Steven Tyler*
- *Kimberley Stewart: daughter of Rod Stewart*
- *Stella McCartney: daughter of Sir Paul McCartney*
- *Amy Winehouse: daughter of London cab driver Mitch Winehouse*
- *Lisa Marie Presley: daughter of Elvis Presley*

ENTERTAINING KIDS

There must be many fathers around the country who have experienced the cruellest, most crushing rejection of all: their children have ended up supporting the wrong team.
Nick Hornby

Keeping kids amused can often be the task of the dad. This is especially hard when it's wet or when your kids are bored by the same old routines of DVDs, electronic games and homework. That's when you need to swing into action with your surprising store of dad-only magic tricks, science experiments and make and do activities. Read on for more ideas.

🚗 DAD TRICKS AND ILLUSIONS 🚗

THE SEVERED FINGER

More of an illusion than a trick, but effective all the same. Get a matchbox, cut a slit out of the bottom of the sleeve along half its length and a hole in the bottom of the internal box. Put some cotton wool soaked in red food dye in the box and offer to show the contents to an unsuspecting child. As you prepare to open the box, slide the middle finger of your supporting hand into the hole. Wait for the screams.

THE SEVERED THUMB

Crook your thumbs and place your left index finger on the crooked joint of your left thumb. Then bang your thumbs together so that the lower part of the right thumb appears to be part of the same digit as the upper part of the left. Do this close to a small child and you can produce a satisfying scream.

THE CARROT AND THE TRICK

Come up with three simple sums ('What's $3+6$?' etc). Ask them to your 'victim' and then ask them to name a vegetable. The chances are they will say carrot, so write this down on a piece of paper and get ready to show it to them. If they say something else, move on quickly to the next one, which is . . .

MILKY, MILKY

Get them to say the word milk five times quickly. Then ask them, 'What do cows drink?' Hopefully they'll say 'milk'. If they say 'water' it's time to practise your disappearing trick.

EGGS-TRAORDINARY

Eggs are incredibly fragile, aren't they? But if you judge an experiment just right you can demonstrate exactly how strong eggs can be. It's all about the position.

Egg in a box. Put a box of half a dozen uncooked eggs on the floor (putting a tea towel down first if you're on carpet). Make sure they are standing straight upright. Then place a book on top of the eggs. Get your children to place one book each on the eggs, continuing the tower until your nerve gives out or the eggs break. You'll be amazed how high the tower can grow before they do.

Ooh – I could crush an egg. This one is better outdoors: get your child to hold an egg lengthways and squeeze to try to break the egg. If you're holding the ends it's almost impossible (though not actually impossible, so don't let them wear their best clothes). The shell of the egg is incredibly strong and can withstand incredible pressure exerted on the ends. Tap the sides and the yolk's on you.

WHO'S HARRY WORTH?

No, we didn't know either. This is a dad's trick from the previous generation of dads, popularised by the comic Harry Worth. It involves standing next to a shop window in which your reflection is clearly visible (a mirrored wardrobe works even better), so that half of your body is obscured. Lift your visible leg and arm and the reflection will do the same, giving watching children a sight of you doing a '*Matrix*'-like mid air frozen jump.

I'M WEARING A WIG

The skin on your scalp is just loose enough to allow you to convince your kids that you are in fact wearing a hairpiece. Grab your hair firmly at the top with one hand and gently your hair backwards and forwards. It will appear to 'slide' around, causing much laughter and deep suspicion that you are, in fact, a slap-head in disguise.

ERIC MORECAMBE'S BAG

Another old classic. Take a paper bag, holding it with the first and third fingers of your hand and the middle finger concealed behind it. Pretend to throw an object up in the air and hold the opened bag out to 'catch' the object. Leave enough time for it to 'drop' and then flick the back of the bag with your hidden middle finger. It sounds exactly like the object dropping into the bag and your audience will be agog when they see there's nothing there.

🚗 THINGS TO MAKE 🚗

Make and do are two of the key words in any dad's arsenal. The degree of ambition you employ depends largely on your creative skills and your children's patience levels. There's nothing worse than a dad who takes over building the train set because the kids 'can't get it right'. Here are some simple ideas that anyone can tackle.

STREET SCENE

You will need: paper, round-nosed scissors, sticky tape, individual variety-box type cereal boxes, a medium sized cardboard box, colouring pens, poster paints and brushes, sponges, and PVA glue.

Method: This is a multi-stage project that will ultimately give your children a great play mat for toy cars. Take a medium sized cardboard box and cut it down the four corners so you have a flat cross shape. Draw the roads and other features on the cardboard and work together to paint the landscape. Then cover the cereal boxes in craft paper and decorate these individually as buildings, before sticking them down to the surface. Finally, add finishing touches like trees or hedges, using the sponges cut up and soaked in paint. Once the scene is finished and dry it's ready to go. When you've finished playing, fold the sides of the box back up and stick tape in each corner so it's easier to store.

HELICOPTERS WITH PAPERCLIPS

You will need: card, round-nosed scissors, and medium sized paperclips.

Method: Cut the card into strips that are 10 × 30cm approx. Halfway along the strip (5cm in) cut down about 10cm. Fold the two flaps of card at the top in opposite directions so they are like the rotors of a helicopter. Place the paper clip at the bottom of the 'helicopter' as ballast. Find somewhere high but safe to fly them from and let them go.

For more make and do activities see pages 100 and 102.

🚗 SIMPLE SCIENCE 🚗

GROW YOUR OWN CRYSTALS

You will need: two jam jars, bicarbonate of soda, a saucer, a length of wool and two paperclips

Method: Fill the jam jars with hot water and stir in about 5tsp of bicarbonate of soda (until no more will dissolve). Put the jars in a warm place, on either side of the saucer. Cut one metre of wool and fix a paperclip to each end of it; put one end in each jar so the paperclip sits on the bottom. Leave the jars undisturbed for 7–10 days. Eventually crystals will grow along the wool and columns may form between the wool and the saucer.

What's happening? The wool soaks up the solution, then the water evaporates to leave the bicarb crystals behind.

MAKE A SUNDIAL

You will need: a stick, modelling clay, stones or chalk and a clock

Method: Start early in the day. Put the stick upright in the clay in a sunny spot on a patio or path. As the day goes by, mark where the shadow falls every hour using the stones or chalk. Try to mark 12 hours.

What's happening? The earth moves constantly around the sun, so for thousands of years people and animals have used the sun to tell the time.

Pocket fact

The earliest known surviving sundial is an Egyptian shadow clock of green schist dating from around 800BC.

FOAMING VOLCANO

You will need: a small plastic bottle, vinegar, washing-up liquid, red food dye, bicarbonate of soda and tissue

Method: Decorate the bottle so it looks like a volcano. Half fill the bottle with vinegar. Add a squirt of washing-up liquid and a drop of the food colouring, swirl the bottle to mix it and put it in a large baking tray. Put a heaped teaspoon of bicarbonate of soda into a small twist of tissue and place the tissue inside the bottle. Sit back and wait for the red lava to come pouring out.

What's happening? The vinegar (acetic acid) and bicarbonate of soda (alkali) mix together. This creates carbon dioxide – a gas which reacts with the washing-up liquid to make foam.

FUN WITH BALLOONS

You will need: some balloons, a strong rectangular tray and some sticky tape

Method: The simplest science trick with a balloon is static electricity. Rub a balloon on a jumper and then stick it to a wall or ceiling. But there's a lot more fun to be had from the simple balloon: try taking four balloons and sticking them to the underside of a strong tray – preferably metal. Make sure they are spread out in each of the four corners and taped in place. Then place the balloons on the floor and stand carefully on the tray. Get your weight evenly distributed and they should hold you without popping.

What's happening? Though the balloons aren't strong, they are working like the eggs in the experiment above, distributing the load over a wide surface area and therefore coping with the extra pressure.

CENTRIFUGAL FORCE

You will need: a small plastic bucket, a piece of rope and some water

Method: This is an outdoor-only experiment. Tie the rope to the handle of the bucket and half-fill the bucket with water. Then clear a decent space around you and swirl the bucket around in a circle using the rope. If you get up to a decent speed and keep your spinning fairly constant, the water will stay in the bucket.

What's happening? This is an example of centrifugal force. The water isn't flying out of the bucket because the g-force exerted on it as it spins is so great.

Pocket tip 🍺

Unless you are really clever or using really big sheets of paper, you cannot fold paper in half any more than seven times. Get your kids to try – they'll be at it for hours.

🚗 TEN INDOOR WAYS TO AMUSE 🚗 YOUR CHILDREN

Bank holidays, wet Sundays and sick days are times when your child's patience can start to stretch. Ease the burden – and the amount of time spent in front of the TV – with these family-friendly indoor pastimes:

1. **Pirates**. A rainy day classic – for this game you will need cushions, a sofa, chairs, plenty of cleared space and no low-lying valuables. The idea is to create a circle of 'stepping stones' around the floor so that it is possible to do a complete circuit of the room without touching the carpet. You all run around the circuit clambering over chairs, sofas and cushions until someone (normally you) loses concentration and puts a foot on the carpet. At that moment you are eaten by sharks and you're out. Continue until someone wins or everyone's dizzy.

2. **Shadow puppets**. You need an angle poise desk lamp, two hands and a lot of imagination for this one. Shine the lamp on a large, light-coloured wall and put your hand in the beam of light so that you cast a shadow on the wall. By shaping your hand you will be able to create a range of animal profiles – easy ones to practise are birds (both hands joined by interlocking thumbs) and an elephant (one hand, using middle finger as trunk, thumb as tusk and crooked index finger as eye). Practice makes perfect. If you get bored, buy a kitten and get it to chase the shadow of your hand on the wall instead. That's a recipe for hours of fun. Obviously it will also need looking after though.

3. **Sock puppet theatre**. If you've got some (clean) odd socks in your drawer, don't just bin them. A bit of inventiveness, some felt shapes and some PVA glue will turn even the rankest old sock into a puppet. Add a bit more interest by making little costumes for the puppets and you've got everything you need for a show.

4. **Cardboard box telly**. A variation on the above theme, this is always a good one when you've just bought something big – like a TV, clearly, but also a microwave or computer. Cut out a screen on one side of the box and then get the kids to draw a variety of backgrounds to go inside the box. Depending on the size of the box, you can either

use puppets as 'actors', or get the kids to climb inside and pretend to be reading the news or forecasting the weather.

Pocket tip 🍺

If you want cardboard boxes for make and do sessions, you can get good strong boxes for free from DIY stores.

5. **Treasure hunt**. Simple, but with some preparation needed. Write a series of clues, each of which lead the 'hunters' around the house to a follow-up clue. After five or six clues you should give them some treasure – sweets or snacks work well. Don't make the clues too obscure and keep them easy to reach.

6. **Carpet cricket**. This is another wet weather favourite, but it also requires a playing area that's free of valuables and breakables. It works best on a wooden or tiled floor, but most carpets are ok too. You need a ruler and a ping pong ball. All participants take part on their knees to limit the crashing around. The rules are similar to normal cricket – you have a wicket and fielders, but there is no running: only a series of targets with associated scores.

7. **TV guide charades**. A big part of childhood Christmases, this is simply a version of the parlour game in which the charades are chosen out of the TV listings. The rules are the same – without speaking or using verbal clues, each participant explains the number of words in the title of a film or TV show and then mimes each word in turn, sometimes breaking down those words into syllables if required. The winner is the one with the most correct guesses.

8. **Flying saucers**. This is a great one for toddlers. Scoop up the child in your arms like a fork-lift truck, holding their legs where the thigh joins the knee in each hand so they can rest their back against your chest. Stick your thumbs up in the air like two joysticks and let them grip these to control the

speed and direction of the spaceship as you go around the
room. Exhausting, but fun.

9. **Mirror man (and Simon says)**. Two versions of the
same thing – one visual, one verbal. The mirror man is a
game where you stand opposite someone and copy, in
mirror image, everything he or she does until you make a
mistake, at which point you need to swap. 'Simon says' is a
game where you give instructions that must be followed,
such as 'Simon says jump on the spot', but only if they are
prefixed by 'Simon says . . .'. An instruction without
Simon's say-so is to be ignored and if you don't ignore it,
you're out.

10. **Post-it questions**. Write the names of various characters
on sticky notes – real or fictional which all the children
will know – and stick each name to the forehead of each
participating child. They then need to find out who their
person is by asking questions – they should only be given
yes or no answers to keep the game going.

Pocket tip 🍺

*Make maths fun by making words with the numbers. Type in
the combinations below, and turn the calculator the wrong
way round. Your kids will show them to all their friends at school
the next day.*

- *Shell = 77345*
- *Boil = 7108*
- *Giggle = 376616*
- *Less = 5537*
- *Obesehog = 60435390*
- *Hollie = 317704*
- *Goose = 35006*
- *Bobsleigh = 461375909*

🚗 **CLASSIC BOARD GAMES** 🚗

Even the most enterprising dad needs some help when it comes
to entertaining the kids. Keep a good stock of board games around

and you'll never be short of amusement. Here are some of the best:

- Games for improving manual dexterity and hand-eye coordination: Operation; Buckaroo; pick-up-sticks; Twister.

- Games for improving concentration and logic: Chess; Risk; backgammon.

- Games for improving deductive skills: Cluedo; Guess Who?

- Games for budding ruthless capitalists: Monopoly.

CLASSIC CARD GAMES

A pack of cards is a good investment for rainy days. As well as being the basic building material for a house of cards, they're actually surprisingly fun to play with. Here are some simple games to get your kids started:

Snap. The simplest and possibly best card game ever invented. Each player is dealt the same number of cards as the pack is divided up equally. They then take it in turns to lay a card down. As soon as two cards of the same type are laid down consecutively, the first person to shout 'SNAP!' gets to keep the pile of cards that have accrued. The winner is the person with the most cards at the end.

Pontoon. Each player is dealt two cards and must decide whether to 'stick' – ie keep the cards they have, or 'twist', ie take another card from the deck as they seek to get as close as possible to a score of 21 points on the cards. Aces count as both one and 11. If a player accrues a score over 21, they are bust and out of the game. The best hand is 21 exactly with five cards.

Uno. A combination of card game and board game, this is a fast and frantic game that features a set of cards with different instructions on them, which impact not on the holder of the cards, but on the next person in turn, who may have to pick up cards. The action switches direction at the drop of a card and the winner is the one who gets rid of all their cards successfully. A great introduction to cards for the very young.

🚗 DADS' JOKES 🚗

When it comes to telling jokes, dads get a pretty bad press and you can see why, judging by the following examples:

- On his relationship: 'I'm the head of the family. But your mother is the neck – she always decides which way we go.'

- On hearing an ambulance: 'He won't sell many ice creams going at that speed!'

- On hearing a fire engine: 'Someone's got more fire than they need!'

- On passing a graveyard: 'I hear people are dying to get in there.'

- On carving the Sunday roast: 'I don't know what you lot are having.'

- On the subject of his best gift ever: 'A hard-boiled egg. You can't beat it.'

🚗 QUICK FIXES 🚗

Top ten must-see films for kids
We've all got our personal favourites, but no collection is complete without these terrific flicks:

1. **Chitty-Chitty Bang Bang**. *Caution advised as the child catcher scene can induce nightmares – as can Dick Van Dyke's singing.*
2. **Monsters Inc**. *Just about the most intelligent and inventive film for kids ever written.*
3. **Toy Story**. *A great morality tale about friendship and trust and filled with little 'in' jokes.*
4. **Mary Poppins**. *See above for advice on Dick Van Dyke, but otherwise this is a gem, with probably the best songs in a kids' musical.*

5. **A Night at the Museum**. *A modern classic that's great for kids of age seven upwards. A little bit scary and violent, but terrific fun with a real family feel.*

6. **The Railway Children**. *'Daddy, my Daddy'. Enough said. Anyone who watches this film without crying has no heart.*

7. **The Wizard of Oz**. *A bit overlong, with a very scary witch, but the story has been imitated so often your kids deserve to see the original. Visually stunning.*

8. **The Jungle Book**. *Ok, so it would send Kipling spinning in his grave, but it's the best standard Disney animation with some great voices, songs and action.*

9. **The Muppets' Christmas Carol**. *Many educated people still regard this as Michael Caine's finest film. It's an absolute must for Christmas Eve – watch out for the singing vegetables.*

10. **Willy Wonka and the Chocolate Factory**. *This is the original Gene Wilder version from the 1970s and it's a bit odd. But then Roald Dahl was a bit odd, which is why kids love his books. Probably the best film version of a Dahl classic (with* Matilda *a close second).*

Top five fancy dress ideas a dad can manage

Fancy dress parties can be a bit of a creative challenge, even for the most artistic dad. Here are some quick-fix costumes that will get you through in the event of a fancy dress emergency:

1. **Knight**. To make a knight's tunic, take a piece of material about 1.5m × 50cm and fold it along the middle. Cut a square hole big enough for your child's head to go through. Draw a design on the front – a big red cross usually does the trick – and use a belt to keep it together around the midriff. It doesn't matter if it hangs a bit long as that's how they wore them in olden days. Cut a sword and shield shape out of cardboard and cover them in kitchen foil, sticking down with tape.

2. **Car**. Get a good-sized cardboard box (around 70cm × 50cm size and 50cm deep) and draw a basic car outline – windows, headlights, doors etc. Cut out a hole in the sunroof big enough for your child's head to go through and holes in the side windows for their arms. Paint the body of the car, then cut out, paint and stick on some wheels.

3. **Wizard/witch**. Take a black bin bag and cut out holes for arms and head. Decorate the bin bag with a silver or gold craft pen – draw some moons, stars and broomsticks. Next take a large sheet of black craft paper and make it into a cone. Trim off the excess so that the cone is round at its widest part and decorate it in the same style as the bin bag. Dress your child in the bin bag with a belt around the midriff, using the cone as a hat.

4. **Mummy**. Take a roll of good quality toilet paper and wrap it around your child. Work in sections and stick them together with tape. Do the arms and legs first, then the body, and then finally the head. Make sure it's not too tight and don't worry if some bits look ragged or hang down: it all adds to the effect. This isn't a good one to go for on a wet Halloween.

5. **Dog**. Good for girls, this one. You need a pair of white leggings, a white long-sleeved top and a white swimming cap. Dress your child in all of the above and then cut out some black cardboard spots to stick all over the costume. Cut out two doggy ears from black card and stick them to the swimming cap. Finally, cut out a tail. You'll need some face paint to give her a face of black spots, whiskers and a nice black nose.

Ten steps to the perfect party

Parties are a lot of fun for kids of all ages. But they can often be the source of much stress for the parents and helpers. Ease the pre-party tension with these helpful hints:

1. **Be organised**. Don't run out on the morning of the party to gather all the food, party bag ingredients and accessories. Make a list and get everything well in advance.

2. **Be calm**. Even if you are excited about the party yourself, don't be tempted to get your child worked up into a frenzy of excitement. Organise something calm and distracting for them to do while you make the final preparations on the big day.

3. **Control it**. Keeping a tight rein on the party is the difference between controlled chaos and, well, chaos. Set aside one room of the house (or a hired hall) for the party, clear it of all ornaments, valuables and electrical items and make sure none of the little blighters escape.

4. **Start on time**. When you give out the invites, tell other parents when you'll be kicking off and stick to that. If little Lucia misses out on pass the parcel that's her own silly fault – you've got to pander to the masses or you'll have a riot on your hands. Make it a lunchtime or early afternoon party – early evening dos are full of angry kids well past their nap time.

5. **Play good games**. Don't over-complicate things with magic, dancing, clowns or discos. Little kids want three things from a party – crap food, good games and a decent bag to take away. You need to make sure they are satisfied. This means pass the parcel (with a gift on every layer), musical statues and musical chairs. In other words, make sure you've got something that plays music.

6. **Keep the food coming**. The nutritional value of party food can be questionable. But even if the kids expect plenty of finger food and snacks, there's no reason you can't make it healthy and fun. Chunks of cheese, carrot and celery sticks, plenty of dips, crackers, breadsticks and wholemeal soldiers will keep the party munching, while limiting the sugary snacks will help to avoid too many hyper (or nauseous) kids racing around the party on a sugar rush.

7. **Don't miss it**. You can spend the whole party racing around, peeling cling film off plastic bowls and cleaning up sick and then realise that your child has opened all their

presents while you were out of the room. Get some help in to do the running around – and to hold the video camera if you want a record of the day. You should be with your child, enjoying the fun.

8. **Finish on time**. If you start at midday, aim to be done by 2.30pm, otherwise the kids will be out of control and you'll be dead on your feet. They'll have had enough by then anyway.

9. **Send them home happy**. Give all the kids a party bag with a bit of cake, a few penny sweets, and pocket money toys. Don't put in a balloon or any toys unsuitable for the age range – and don't overload the bag with sugary treats.

10. **Don't sweat the small stuff**. Make the whole day easier by using decorative paper cloths, plates and cups. You can simply bin the whole lot when you're done.

MAN OF THE HOUSE

Hatred of domestic work is a natural and admirable result of civilisation.
Rebecca West

Home is where the heart is, but it's also where the man of the house is expected to deal with any squeaky hinges, wobbly tables and creepy crawlies. It also helps if you know how to deal with basic household mishaps. This chapter explains how to be a domestic god.

🚗 UNWANTED PESTS 🚗

How to . . . catch a bird trapped indoors

1. Take some fabric, such as net curtains or a towel. Hold the fabric outstretched and follow the bird around the room quietly and without making sudden movements.

2. When the bird lands in a vulnerable position with plenty of space around it, toss the light fabric over the bird and gather it gently around it.

3. Get it to a window as soon as you can and release it immediately.

Pocket fact 🚩
Much of the dust in a house is made up of the discarded skin cells of the inhabitants . . . nice.

DEALING WITH SPIDERS AND OTHER CREEPY-CRAWLIES

The best way to keep unwelcome guests out is to stop them getting in. Seal gaps in skirting boards and window frames with silicone sealant and make sure you keep all bed linen clean – give it a regular hot wash. Clean up any spillages of food immediately and make sure all opened food packets are stored in cupboards or sealed.

Spiders

You need a sheet of stiff paper and a wide-rimmed glass or mug. In a swift and steady movement, place the glass over the spider, trapping it underneath. Then gently slide the paper between the mug and the surface, so that you've got it safely trapped inside. Turn the glass upright, keeping a hand over the paper, and then take the spider outside and release it well clear of the house.

Pocket tip 🍺

It is believed that spiders have an aversion to horse chestnuts (conkers). If you place a conker in each corner of the room it will apparently keep the little blighters at bay.

Bedbugs

Make sure your bed linen is cleaned on a hot wash and that it is changed regularly. Use a mattress topper. Keep the area around and underneath the bed clear of dust and other mess. If you get an infestation, call in the experts as they are a pain to shift.

Fleas

Use a decent flea killer on your pets – these are available from supermarkets or vets. If your pet's bed is infested, destroy the bed as you'll never get it completely clear.

Clothes moths

First of all, don't keep too many clothes in your wardrobe. Hang only the clothes you're going to wear that season, storing all other clothes in plastic under-bed storage packs, preferably vacuum sealing them first. If you do get any moth infestation, have the affected clothes dry cleaned. Don't put dirty wool clothes or cashmere into a wardrobe.

DEALING WITH MICE AND RATS

Prevention is better than cure when it comes to rodent infestation. Although mice in particular are adept at getting through small crevices, your best bet to keep them out of the house is to block any little cracks or holes in the perimeter wall of your property, unless they are necessary for ventilation.

- Check pipe work, brickwork and around doors and windows for possible points of entry.

- Keep all food in cupboards or storage boxes, and don't leave anything standing around – such as pet food.

- Sweep the kitchen floor regularly to ensure that all food waste is cleared up.

If all of the above doesn't prevent mice or rates from getting in, you'll need to set traps. These can be preferable to poison as a poisoned rodent can crawl back into a loft space or wall cavity to die, leaving you with a smelly and potentially expensive clean-up operation. If you're going for a trap you'll need to decide whether to use traditional or humane traps.

With a traditional trap you'll need to remove the dead mouse and discard it carefully so it doesn't leave a smell, and with a humane variety you'll have to take the mouse right out of your garden before releasing it, otherwise it'll just come straight back.

Pocket tip 🍺

Never use rat or mouse poison in an area where pets and children can get access to it.

Key household inventions and their dates

- 1500BC – Glass
- 600BC – Sewerage
- 220BC – Gunpowder
- 130BC – Concrete
- 1281AD – Spectacles
- 1447 – Printing press
- 1589 – Flushable toilet
- 1835 – Electric generator
- 1838 – Computer
- 1839 – Photography
- 1866 – Refrigerator
- 1871 – Vacuum cleaner
- 1877 – Telephone
- 1933 – Television
- 1945 – Microwave oven
- 1959 – Video recorder
- 1985 – Personal computer
- 1990 – Internet
- 1993 – Pentium processor
- 1993 – DVDs
- 2001 – iPod
- 2003 – Hybrid car
- 2008 – iPhone

How to . . . light a fire

1. If you're laying an open fire you'll need to be sure the fire basket is clean and clear of built-up ash, as air needs to circulate all around the fire.

2. Take some newspaper and tear each page in half, making some stick-like twists. Position these twists of paper in the heart of your fire.

3. Take about 10 bits of dry kindling (pieces of bare wood about the size of a chocolate bar) and lean these against the newspaper twists as if you're making a wooden tepee.

4. Then take two or three substantial split logs and rest them against the structure.

5. Using a long splint or gas gun, light the paper at the heart of the fire in a few places.

6. Stand some more logs near the fire, ready to go on. The warmer the logs are, the more they're likely to burn well without smoking.

7. Wait 12 hours before cleaning out the fire basket prior to setting another fire. The cinders and ashes will continue to smoulder for a long time.

Pocket tip 🍺

If the fire's giving you difficulty, use firelighters in the 'heart' of the fire to get things going.

🚗 CLEANING 🚗

Top ten household stains and how to remove them

Where there are kids there are stains, but not every spill means an expensive trip to the furniture showroom – there are plenty of household remedies for getting rid of nasty stains.

Pocket tip 🍺

Only one stain is almost impervious to removal: milk spilt on carpet. If you catch it early enough, you may remove it with white vinegar, but otherwise you'll need a professional cleaner or a new carpet.

Try the following:

1. **Candle wax on the carpet**. To remove candle wax from a carpet, first dig off the top layer of dried wax with a metal teaspoon. Then take a warm iron and a sheet of brown paper and place the paper over the wax stain, gently ironing the paper to lift the grease from the stain and soak it into the paper. Stick with it for a few minutes and the whole stain will eventually lift out, leaving no greasy residue.

2. **Grass stains on fabric**. Remove these from non-washable fabrics by gently rubbing with a cloth dipped into a paste of cream of tartar and water.

3. **Blood stains on clothes**. Assuming that these were acquired legally, you can remove them by soaking the affected fabric in cool, salted water. Otherwise report immediately to the nearest police station and give yourself up . . .

4. **Red wine on a carpet**. A red wine stain on the carpet can be removed by dousing the affected area with white wine. Though it seems a further waste of wine, it does work wonders.

5. **Food stains on a carpet**. Minor food stains on carpets and non-washable fabrics can be treated by rubbing half a freshly chopped potato on the affected area.

6. **Chewing gum on a rug/carpet**. Freeze the gum with an ice cube and then chip away the solidified residue with a knife, taking care not to cut into the carpet fibres.

7. **Ink stains on clothes**. Rub the stain with a ripe tomato, then wash as normal.

8. **Urine stains on clothing/carpets**. A big problem with children's clothing, for obvious reasons. Use salt to soak up any excess liquid on a carpet and then treat with white vinegar.

9. **Rust stains on clothes**. These can be removed by rubbing them with lemon juice and then washing as normal.

10. **Tougher stains**. The toughest stains to remove are those which have been washed once then dried in. If none of the above treatments work, and you can't remove the stain using a stain-removal product or bleach, then go to a dry cleaner and see what they recommend.

Pocket tip 🍺

The acetic acid in vinegar is a great cleaning agent — it's especially good at cutting through grime and grease. A few drops added to warm water makes a perfectly good floor or window cleaning product. You can also use lemon juice if you're not keen on the idea of your house smelling like a chip shop.

How to . . . use the washing machine

Whether your washing machine is a modern mechanical marvel or an old crock that sounds as if it's going to break through the floor every time it goes into a spin cycle, it will almost certainly be operated by the same simple rules:

1. **Don't overload it**. If you put so much stuff in the machine that you have to wedge it in tight just so you can get the door closed, you've overloaded it. This means nothing will wash well and you'll probably end up with a damaged drum. The drum should never be more than three-quarters full.

2. **Find out where to put the powder or liquid**. Read the instructions on the carton or bottle. If in doubt, add the detergent to the largest compartment of the tray at the top of the machine. Don't overdo the detergent otherwise everything will come out needing another rinse.

3. **Don't mix colours and whites**. Even if you're washing older clothes, it's good practice to keep dark clothes away from light ones to avoid colour run.

4. **Choose the right programme**. The machine will have a variety of temperature settings. The lower the temperature, the gentler the wash, so if you're washing delicate fabrics, do it at 40°C or lower. Modern machines and detergents claim they can give good cleaning at 30°C. A 90°C wash is the equivalent of a boil wash for tough stains and strong fabrics such as bed sheets.

5. **Remove tough stains first**. Use a stain removal spray or roll-on to break down tougher stains before your put them in the machine. It'll save you having to wash again and again.

Pocket fact

As well as being fantastically difficult to iron, women's shirts (blouses) always have the buttons on the left. Men's have buttons on the right.

Being a parent is a big responsibility; one of life's greatest things . . . a pain in the arse.
Noel Gallagher

Ten Dads in Literature

- *King Lear* in King Lear *(William Shakespeare)*
- *Atticus Finch* in To Kill a Mockingbird *(Harper Lee)*
- *Arthur Weasley* in the Harry Potter *books (JK Rowling)*
- *Mr Bennet* in Pride and Prejudice *(Jane Austen)*
- *Joe Gargery* in Great Expectations *(Charles Dickens)*
- *Michael Henchard* in The Mayor of Casterbridge *(Thomas Hardy)*
- *John Wheelwright's father* in A Prayer for Owen Meany *(John Irving)*
- *Lord Asriel* in the His Dark Materials *trilogy (Philip Pullman)*
- *Mr. Darling from* Peter Pan *(J.M. Barrie)*
- *Victor Frankenstein* in Frankenstein *(Mary Shelley)*

IN THE GARDEN

Gardening is the new rock and roll.
Ali Ward

Dads can excel in the garden – it's the part of the home that you're usually allowed to call your own. Nothing quite beats a leisurely afternoon spent mowing the lawn or tinkering in the shed. So get your best gardening clothes on and head outside with these great tips for making the most of your land.

🚗 LAWN CARE 🚗

To get your lawn into good shape you need some serious commitment, but it's not necessarily as back-breaking a job as you might think.

Mow but not too low. Mow your lawn from the spring to the autumn with a fairly high blade. Doing this little and often will lessen the likelihood of moss build-up on the lawn.

Sprinkle, don't tinkle. One of the biggest mistakes the lawn enthusiast can make is to think that lawns will survive on rainwater alone. This isn't true – if you're in a dry spell, you need to give your lawn a really good drink of water to stop it going brown and patchy.

Keep it clear and neat. Get rid of great big nutrient-hungry weeds like dandelions by plucking them out of the lawn by hand – being sure to get the root as well. Use a lawn rake to gather up dead wood, leaves and other rotting substances, and try to keep the moss build-up to a minimum – remember it's better to have a bald patch in the short term if it prevents moss from taking over your whole patch.

> ## *Understanding plants – a glossary*
>
> **Annual** – *a plant that lives for just one year.*
> **Biennial** – *a plant that produces flowers/fruit in its second year.*
> **Cutting** – *a section of a plant removed to grow another plant.*
> **Dead-head** – *to remove the flowers of a plant before they go to seed.*
> **Hardy** – *strong enough to be grown outside all year.*
> **Herbaceous** – *a plant that dies back every autumn.*
> **Mulch** – *a layer of material (usually organic, like bark chips) which goes around the roots of a plant to protect it from frost.*
> **Perennial** – *a plant that grows and/or flowers every year.*
> **Succulent** – *a plant with thick leaves that are good for storing water.*

🚗 THE PERFECT BONFIRE 🚗

You should build a bonfire in the same way you'd build an indoor fire, starting from a small and fairly tight heart of easily flammable material, such as paper or very dry wood. Once this heart is burning well you can add pretty much anything to your fire and it will burn it. This is even true for wet leaves, though they are liable to create an awful lot of smoke.

Dig a pit for your fire, or at the very least, make sure it is well away from any other vegetation so it can't spread and cause unnecessary damage. Look up as well: if there are any trees hanging over your bonfire think again – the flames may not look very fierce at the start, but in full flow they'll be leaping six feet (1.8m) into the air and you don't want the fire to get out of control.

Here are a few more dos and don'ts:

Do: Keep adding little and often. Break items up before burning and check for non-combustible items, such as aerosol cans and toxic paint.

Do: Stay in attendance. Never leave a bonfire to burn without supervision.

Do: Check whether there are any restrictions on bonfires in your neighbourhood and let your neighbours know that you are having a fire if they've left windows open or washing on the line.

Don't: Build a fire then wait a few days to light it. You'll end up with a barbecue featuring whichever animal has chosen to sleep inside – likely candidates include cats, dogs, foxes and hedgehogs.

Pocket tip 🍺

Never use any fire-lighting fluid or petrol to get a bonfire going. It's a recipe for disaster. If the fire won't light, it's because your raw materials are too damp or because it's too windy. Abandon the idea and try again later.

🚗 DEALING WITH MOLES, INSECT 🚗 INFESTATIONS AND OTHER PESTS

MOLES

These are a gardener's worst nightmare – they pop up in spring and autumn and can dig tunnels at a rate of 4m an hour. Methods for discouraging moles range from sinking milk bottles into a mole run, to crumbling dried eucalyptus leaves into it. These tips will only divert the moles (possibly into your neighbour's garden) and the most effective way to stop moles is to trap them – you can get traps from hardware stores. Fumigation (gassing) also works, but it can be a messy and potentially harmful activity. Ant powder is a less toxic and sometimes effective alternative to gas.

BEES

If bees nest in your garden you're pretty much stuck with them, but this may depend on the type of bee you've got. Check with the council's environmental health team, but don't remove the nest yourself.

WASPS

Wasps' nests near houses are usually destroyed by the council or private firms. Don't attempt to tackle a wasps' nest yourself as they can be potentially dangerous. Again, you should get in touch with environmental health as they can usually provide a cheap and effective solution.

ANTS

There are plenty of poisons, powders and other products that claim to get rid of ants – don't go for the cheapest. To stop ants getting into the house, sprinkle ant powder around outside walls and make sure any holes in the brickwork/woodwork are filled. If you can find the nest, pour boiling water directly onto it. If not, put powder down, which the ants will then carry back to the nest.

FLIES, ETC

A lot of insects are attracted by compost, stagnant water or piles of domestic rubbish. Keeping the area near your home litter-free will cut the risk of infestation.

🚗 WHAT TO DO IN THE GARDEN 🚗 AND WHEN TO DO IT

SPRING

This is the time to prune climbing plants and shrubs and to feed them in preparation for the year's growth. You should also sow grass seed now and start planting out the majority of your vegetables and annuals.

SUMMER

Water everything regularly, including the lawn. Dead-head flowers that have started to die back and feed those that are still to flower. Put spring flowering bulbs into storage.

AUTUMN

Keep the garden tidy by clearing up dead leaves – pay particular attention to clearing leaves from ponds and guttering – use mesh or netting to protect if necessary. Plant out any late season vegetables and salads.

WINTER

Use fleece or similar material to protect susceptible plants from the cold. Prune fruit trees and roses. Bring any particularly frost-sensitive plants indoors. While indoors, sow seed for the following spring.

Top ten outdoor ways to amuse your children

Entertaining your kids outside has the double benefit of filling their little lungs with fresh air and allowing them to run around without breaking things. The following outdoor activities are all 'garden' games, which can be played in an average-sized space:

1. **French cricket**. So-called because it's not really cricket. But it is good fun and it requires a lot less kit to play than the normal variety of the game. You need a cricket bat and a tennis ball. The batter holds the bat in front of their legs and the other players stand in a circle around them. One person bowls the ball underarm and tries to hit the legs of the batter or get them to hit a catch to the fielders. The batter tries to hit the ball beyond the circle of fielders to score runs. When you're out you swap over. Simple, and yet very French.

2. **Treasure hunt**. You can either transplant the indoor version to the outside world, or turn it into a scavenger hunt where the kids have to bring back items from a list of weeds, bugs, worms, slugs or similar garden pests to gain a prize. The downside could be your kids bringing you a range of rare plants, ripped from the soil, to check if they are weeds or not.

3. **Leaf chase**. Posh kids at public schools used to get sent out every Wednesday afternoon for a paper chase, where some little rogue scattered paper around the British countryside as a way of marking a route for his classmates to follow in an otherwise unremarkable cross-country run. You can put this bizarre practice into reverse every autumn by arming your kids with carrier bags and sending them off to fill them with fallen leaves. The one who fills the most bags is the winner. One tip: get them to wear gloves, as piles of leaves often conceal all sorts of nasty things.

4. **Washing the car**. Ok, so it looks like slave labour, but kids and water do mix. The first thing you need to do is get the kids properly waterproofed. You can get hold of head-to-toe waterproof clothes from camping stores. Then equip the kids with buckets and brushes. They can work on the wheels, sides, front and back of the car while you're doing the roof. Don't leave a young child in charge of a hose or a jet washer unless you're very brave.

5. **Triathlon**. Not a gruelling cycling, swimming, running combo, but a mixture of three garden games played in a tournament. Choose things that are easy to combine – an egg and spoon race, a slow bike race and a dressing up race, for example – as they will all use the same playing area and will require minimal effort to set up.

6. **Putting green**. If you've given up on the idea of a flawless manicured lawn, you could make the ultimate sacrifice and convert it into a putting green. Sink nine plastic flower pots into the lawn and mark out starting positions for each hole. Vary the length and difficulty of some of the holes – see if you can get a dog-leg in there somewhere – and get hold of a cheap putter (boot fairs and charity shops are a decent source of cheap golf kit) and some balls. Hey presto, the next Tiger Woods is in your garden.

7. **The dig**. This works really well with older children if you've got a patch of waste ground or an unused vegetable garden. You need some wooden stakes, some garden twine, a spade, a stiff brush and some trowels. Mark an area one metre square with the twine and stakes and start digging to a depth of 50cm or so. Carry the spoil from the hole away from the site and then let the kids get into the hole and use their trowels to dig further. There will probably be some glass in the soil, so get them to wear thick gloves, but they will almost certainly find some old pottery/crockery and tiles that are worth keeping and cleaning up as 'ancient treasure'.

8. **For the birds**. Feeding wildlife may be a bit of a slow-burner when it comes to outdoor activities, but it can

foster a real love of nature too. Create a dedicated space for wild animal food that's well away from your house, but in full view of a window. You can get the kids to leave bird food, squirrel food, hedgehog treats – even food for badgers and foxes if you want them in your garden. You don't have to buy expensive food hangers – you can make your own fat balls and coconut hangers. Make the experience more interactive by getting hold of a bird spotter's guide and a cheap pair of binoculars for your kids to use while they're indoors.

9. **Picnic**. One of the simplest and most effective ways to use your garden is simply as somewhere to sit and relax with your kids. Lunch eaten outside on a picnic rug always takes on a special dimension, and once the food is finished it also doubles up as a magic carpet or a desert island.

10. **Camping**. A terrific summer diversion, camping doesn't have to be an overnight activity. Just having a tent – or even a table cloth draped over some garden chairs – is enough to keep kids amused for hours as they get absorbed in a totally new environment. See page 93.

And two we never do any more but should resurrect . . .

1. **Conkers**. Though Britain remains steadfastly at the forefront of the world conker movement, many schools have outlawed the (almost) harmless pursuit from the playground. It's the 'almost' part that bothers them – the outside possibility of an eye injury or a broken finger – but frankly there are few better tests of hand/eye coordination. It's also quite marvellous to witness the inventive lengths that children will go to in order to make their conker invincible.

2. **Tin can telephones**. An outdoor activity because of the sheer logistical difficulties of doing it inside the house. You need two clean tin cans and a very long piece of string. Use a bradawl to make a hole in the bottom of the cans, push the string through and tie it off. Then get your child to walk away with one of the cans until the string is taut. Take it in turns to talk through the cans – swap messages, and see how accurately they are taken.

SHEDS

WHY WE NEED THEM

Every man has a shed, even if he doesn't actually own a little musty wooden structure in the garden. The shed is a state of mind, a refuge from the world where he keeps the essential things that everyone else would call junk. Women have handbags for largely the same purpose, but do they get criticised in the same way? I think not.

The point of the shed is illustrated by the variety of its uses – what other space can be an artist's studio, a production line, a writer's study and a bar all in one? Roald Dahl would have been lost without his. It's where we explore our desires and create worlds.

THE SHED SUBSTITUTE

Some of us don't have the space or the inclination for a physical structure, but does that make us anti-shed? Never. We just find other places to make our shed – a study, garage, tool box, drawer of a desk, even a shoe-box under the bed will do the job. As long as it's yours and yours alone it will work.

SHED FACTS

If you are actually set on creating the object of your inner desires in the garden, you need to make sure you're on the level – literally and figuratively. You will need a good solid base to start with, and that may be well compacted soil with a wooden frame on top, or it may be a concrete base poured onto ballast set into the ground, or it may be concrete paving slabs set into a bed of builders' sand. You'll also need to be sure you don't fall foul of planning permission which, in short, means the following:

- Don't exceed 30sqm floor space (or 15sqm if you want to avoid building regulations control).

- Don't have a roof height exceeding 3m (flat roof) or 4m (pitched roof).

- Keep the shed a distance of at least 1m from any boundary.

- Don't buy a shed that uses more than 50% of your garden area.

- Don't use it for sleeping accommodation, install a toilet or run a business from the shed.

- Don't install power yourself unless you are an authorised and competent electrical installer.

- Check other regulations that apply in conservation areas and areas of outstanding natural beauty.

If you exceed or break any of the above conditions, you will almost certainly need planning permission or building control approval. Check with your local authority building control team for more info.

For the shed-head

Shed mania is perfectly understandable, especially when you mix the heady aroma of creosote with the sight of nails in old jam jars. But sheds also have a social function. Australia has seen a massive boom in 'Men's sheds' projects, which are community-based schemes where men gather to chat, share a 'tinnie' and compare saws. It's mildly homoerotic, but an overwhelmingly positive way to get blokes talking to each other. Sheds are here to stay, and we should embrace that fact.

Pocket tip 🍺

Collecting odds and ends in jam jars is one of the greatest joys of shed ownership. But these jars can eat up the space on your shelves. If you screw the lid of the jam jar to the underside of the shelf it will allow you to suspend the jar in mid-air and free up shelf space to use for other things.

CAR KNOW-HOW

No other man-made device since the shields and lances of ancient knights fulfils a man's ego like an automobile.
Lord Rootes

If the above quote wasn't true we wouldn't spend hours cleaning, polishing and nurturing our cars. The car industry wouldn't be a massive and vital part of the world economy. *Top Gear* wouldn't exist. But in all honesty, not many of us actually have a clue when it comes to keeping the damn things on the roads. This chapter gives you all the basics you need to keep your car roadworthy.

🚗 EMERGENCY CAR CARE 🚗

How to . . . jump start a car

If you've got a flat battery, a set of jump leads and another vehicle handy, here's how to jump start a car:

1. Position the cars in such a way that the batteries are close together but the cars are not touching. Switch off the engines, put the cars into first gear, make sure the handbrakes are on fully and then open the bonnets.

2. Take the red jump lead and attach one clamp to the positive terminal of the charged battery and the other to the positive terminal of the flat battery.

3. Clamp the black jump lead to any bare metalwork on the engine frame of the car with the dead battery. Then do the same with the other car. This will earth the charge.

4. You don't need to start both cars at this stage as the charge will flow without turning the engines on. After a short while, try switching on the car with the flat battery.

5. As soon as you get the car with the flat battery working, remove the jump leads in the reverse order to the way to applied them. Do it slowly and one connection at a time.

6. Run the engine with the flat battery for at least twenty minutes to ensure it has got plenty of charge.

Car firsts

- Steam propelled vehicles were the forerunners of modern-day cars. They were first developed in the late 18th century.
- Karl Benz designed the first commercially available modern car in 1887.
- The first Grand Prix was held in 1901 – the cars travelled at an average of 46mph.
- Mercedes pioneered the padded dashboard as a safety feature in 1954.
- Seatbelts were first introduced in the USA in 1963.

How to . . . push start a car

1. Push starting a car will require a team of willing helpers and some good fortune – it won't work if the battery is *completely* dead.

2. You can only push start a car on a flat surface or – ideally – running down a gentle slope. Release the handbrake, put the car into neutral gear and get at least three strong adults to push the car into position.

3. Then get them to push quickly so that the car builds up good momentum – try the ignition at this point and hopefully the car will jump into life.

4. Put it into gear and away you go. Follow step six in how to jump start a car above to ensure the battery is fully recharged.

Pocket tip 🍺

Always resist the temptation to push start a car down a steep hill. It will make the car go faster, but it will be more dangerous and you won't get any volunteers to push it back up again if the attempt fails.

How to . . . change a flat tyre

1. **Be prepared**. A flat tyre is a major headache and your advance planning will make all the difference between a long and humiliating wait for a roadside repairman and a relatively simple process that you should be able to do yourself. Preparation means having the right kit in the car. Number one essential is a decent spare tyre – it's against the law to carry a flat or bald spare tyre, so make sure yours is in good condition. You also need a car jack, a tyre iron (a large cross-shaped wrench) and some WD40-like lubricant.

2. **Make it safe**. Park the car, put on the handbrake and put the car into gear. If you're parked on a slope, put a stone or chock of wood under the wheel diagonally opposite the one you're jacking up to ensure the car doesn't roll forward.

3. **Loosen the wheel**. First take off the hubcap and then use your tyre iron to loosen – but not remove – the lug nuts that hold the wheel to the axle. The nuts will be very stiff at first – they loosen in an anticlockwise direction. If the nuts won't budge, spray some lubricant over them, leave for a minute then try again. Loosen nuts that are directly opposite each other, working round the wheel in sequence.

4. **Jack up the car**. Find the right spot on the car's body for the jack – if you're unclear, your driver's manual will show you. Slowly jack the car up to a height that is sufficient to

remove the flat tyre and put on the new one. Now remove the lug nuts and keep them safe.

5. **Replace the wheel**. Take the wheel off and lay it flat. Put the new wheel into place and reattach it using the lug nuts. Attach them in the same way that you took them off, working around the wheel with opposites. Tighten so that the nuts are secure, but not too tight. Then slowly and carefully release the jack and remove it. Finally, tighten the nuts as firmly and securely as you can, then replace the hubcap.

Pocket tip 🍺

If you're having all your tyres replaced, but one is within the legal limits, get the tyre mechanic to check out your spare and replace it with the legal tyre if necessary.

Who is The Stig?

Despite heavy security, the identity of Top Gear's *tame racing driver 'The Stig' is a constant matter of interest on forums and fan sites around the world. The original Stig was revealed as stunt driver Perry McCarthy, who lost his job after revealing all in his biography. His replacement is believed to be Le Mans driver Ben Collins, but such is the show's shroud of secrecy that the man himself will never reveal his true identity. As a stunt for the show, former Formula one ace Michael Schumacher was once 'revealed' as the white-suited racer.*

🚗 **TRAVELLING WITH CHILDREN** 🚗

Ten tips for surviving car journeys with kids

Car journeys can turn rapidly from a way of getting from A to B to a way of driving you round the bend, if you don't prepare. Follow these tips for an easier ride:

1. Have an emergency bag to hand – this will need to include wipes, tissues, fruit, drinks and sweets.

2. Have some games up your sleeve (see below) or get hold of a portable DVD player.

3. Make it easy for your children to nap. Don't play loud music, and give them soft pillows and a blanket to rest on.

4. Make sure you build in plenty of time and plan enough stops for everyone. A four or five hour journey should have a couple of breaks for visits to the toilet, stretching the legs and getting fresh air. You don't need to spend a fortune at motorway services, just take a break.

5. Take an empty plastic bottle with you just in case you're stuck in traffic and your little boy can't wait to use the loo. There have got to be some advantages of being male!

6. Make sure you've got a full first aid kit in the car just in case of an emergency.

7. If your children don't enjoy time in the car, travel early in the morning or late in the evening when they're naturally sleepy.

8. Keep a carrier bag handy to collect all the rubbish that gets generated over the course of a journey.

9. Don't get stressed yourself – your children will pick up on your own tension, so relax and let the journey take its course.

10. Plan well. If there's traffic chaos, make sure you've got a good map or satellite navigation system to help you plan an alternative route.

CHILD SEATS IN CARS

The laws relating to child seats are fairly complex, but one element is simple – every child of any age at any stage should be belted up in a moving car. Taking that as our basis, there are some key points to consider.

Baby carriers

Seats for babies up to 10kg in weight should be rear-facing. Most babies stay in a rear-facing seat until they are around nine months old. The main problem with these seats is that they can be really bulky, so check out the space in your car before you buy. You'll be surprised at how a baby seat fills up space in even the bigger family cars. Never put a rear-facing baby seat in the front seat of a car with an active passenger airbag. These seats, and the forward-facing varieties available for children up to 13kg (around 15 months old) or bigger will all come with specific fitting instructions. You should get the sales assistant who sells you the seat to talk you through fitting – and try fitting it yourself – before leaving the store. If you buy a new seat online, make sure it comes with full installation instructions.

Pocket tip 🍺

A child seat is definitely not an accessory that you can save money on. Never buy or use a second-hand car seat unless you are absolutely certain that it hasn't been damaged or involved in an accident.

Booster seat

From around four years of age, children can use a booster seat – the exact calculations are based on height and weight. Booster seats are used with the car's seatbelts – which you should check for signs of wear and tear, especially if you drive an older car.

Pocket fact 🏌

In a 30mph crash, an unrestrained child would be thrown forward with a force 30–60 times their body weight.

FITTING A CHILD SEAT

When it comes to actually fitting the seat, you need to follow the following procedure carefully. A badly fitted seat is a potential hazard to everyone in the car:

1. It is really important that you fit the seat according to the manufacturer's instructions. If you don't have any instructions, get them directly from the manufacturer.

2. Pass the seatbelt through the correct section on the seat.

3. If the seatbelt is too short, some seats have an alternative route you can use for the belt. You'll find this marked in the instructions, or possibly marked on the seat itself.

4. As you tighten the seatbelt, you should put your full weight into the seat so that it is held firmly with no slack. The belt should never be twisted.

5. Make sure that the seatbelt buckle is well clear of the edge of the car seat.

6. Once the seat is in place, grab the harness and give the seat a good tug: if it doesn't budge then it is fitted correctly.

7. Sit your child in the seat and tighten the harness, making sure you can get a couple of fingers between the harness and your child. Slacken it a little if it is too tight.

Ten great car games

Playing games in the car is a useful distraction technique. These classics should help the journey zip by:

1. **I-Spy**. *The original and still the best. Good for ages 4+.*

2. **The Alphabet Game**. *Think of a category – films, names, foods etc – and then take it in turns to come up with suggestions, running through the alphabet: 'Apples, bread, cakes . . . etc'. Very good for older children.*

3. **Yes/No**. *Take it in turns to ask questions to which the answers can be anything apart from yes or no.*

4. **Pub bingo**. *If your journey takes in lots of back roads, give your kids simple bingo cards with common pub names on them. The first to spot all their pubs wins a prize.*

5. **Guess the make**. *A good motorway diversion – the children compete to see who's quickest to guess the make of the lorries coming along the opposite lane. Very good for little boys who are truck-mad.*

6. **Number plate acronyms**. *Make up phrases or sayings based on the letters on a number plate. This is a good one to occupy children in traffic jams.*

7. **Yellow car**. *Or green car, or white car – the simplest game of all, looking out for rare colours and shouting out when you spot them.*

8. **Animal, vegetable or mineral**. *Another 'parlour game' that fills time. Someone thinks of an object and can answer questions on it, but only with 'yes and no' answers.*

9. **Landmarks quiz**. *If you're travelling on a pretty familiar route – like taking the kids to their grandparents – set them a quiz with questions that they can answer by spotting sights and landmarks along the way.*

10. **Animal hunt**. *Get the children to look out for animals: award one point for common sights like dogs, cats, sheep and cows, but more for rare sightings. Give a prize at the end.*

🚗 COMMON CAR PROBLEMS 🚗

BRAKES

You can't ignore brake problems. If your dashboard brake warning light comes on, you've got a problem that requires expert help. The brake fluid may be low – and while other fluid loss can be relatively easy to fix yourself, brake fluid should not leak or evaporate. So get it checked out by a mechanic. If you hear a persistent scraping or grinding sound that fades when you brake, your pads are wearing out – if the scraping becomes really pronounced, you're down to metal, which could be really dangerous.

COOLING SYSTEM

If the car is prone to overheating, check the level of coolant in the radiator and if it seems very low when cold, top up with some more distilled water or antifreeze. If the system isn't low on coolant, the problem may lie with the fan or fan belt. Get these checked as they will cause overheating if they're not working properly.

TYRES

You should check the tread of your tyres all over to ensure they are within the legal requirements of 1.6mm minimum across the whole tyre's tread depth. A tread depth of at least 3mm is recommended. You should also keep your tyres inflated to the manufacturer's recommended pressure. This keeps them working longer and will also improve your fuel consumption.

WINDSCREEN

If you get a chip in your windscreen that is not directly within the driver's field of vision and which is smaller in diameter than a 5p coin, you can normally have it repaired for free under the terms of your car insurance. It's a lot less hassle and expense than a replacement. If the wiper blades are in poor condition and aren't cleaning the window well enough, you can replace these yourself. Check your driver's manual for the correct blade size. Lift the wipers away from the car, slide the old blades out from the wiper arms (you may need to detach them from their mounting) and replace with the new blades.

GEARS AND CLUTCH

If your clutch feels loose when you press it lightly, it may need adjusting. If gears don't engage correctly, if you have to force the

car into gear, or if it drops out of gear, you may need a new trans-
mission system.

BATTERY

A decent battery will last for about four to five years. If it starts to
develop a fault, or goes flat regularly for no reason, get it checked
by an expert – car accessory shops will often provide this service
for free. The reason for the flat battery may also be a faulty
alternator. A battery test will show this for sure.

FLUIDS AND FILTERS

As a rule you should check the levels of oil, coolant, washer fluid,
power steering fluid and brake fluid every six weeks or so to
ensure everything is running smoothly. You should replace the
coolant and the oil annually, and replace the oil filter at the same
time. The fuel filter should be replaced every 6,000 miles or every
two years, whichever comes first.

The basic legal requirements for a 'roadworthy' car are:

- A valid, correctly displayed road tax disc
- An MOT
- Legal tyres (see above)
- Insurance
- A safe level of exhaust emissions
- Windscreen washer fluid

Top ten dream cars

1. **SSC Ultimate Aero** (top speed 257mph, 0 to 60 in 2.7 sec)
2. **Bugatti Veyron** (253mph, 0 to 60 in 2.5 sec)
3. **Saleen S7 Twin Turbo** (248mph, 0 to 60 in 3.2 sec)
4. **Koenigsegg CCX** (245mph, 0 to 60 in 3.2 sec)

5. *McLaren F1* (*240mph, 0 to 60 in 3.2 sec*)
6. *Ferrari Enzo* (*217mph, 0 to 60 in 3.4 sec*)
7. *Jaguar XJ220* (*217mph, 0 to 60 in 3.8 sec*)
8. *Pagani Zonda* (*215mph, 0 to 60 in 3.5 sec*)
9. *Lamborghini Murcielago LP640* (*211mph, 0-60 in 3.3 sec*)
10. *Porsche Carerra GT* (*205mph, 0-60 in 3.9 sec*)

The last two of these are by far the cheapest, retailing at a paltry £300,000 each approx.

When a man opens the car door for his wife, it's either a new car or a new wife.
Prince Philip, Duke of Edinburgh

DIY KNOW-HOW

I would be the most content if my children grew up to be the kind of people who think decorating consists mostly of building enough bookshelves.
Anna Quindlen

🚗 WHY DIY? 🚗

DIY is a serious pride issue for a lot of men – as a dad you feel you should be able to take the lead on a range of household tasks. But this gung-ho approach is one of the main reasons behind the 200,000 plus DIY-related hospital cases every year. So before you pick up the jet-powered hammer drill and start knocking lumps out of your home, read this guide to the key skills all dads must master. The first rule of DIY is to start simple. Shelves, pictures and curtain poles are the three basic jobs anyone should be able to manage.

🚗 HANGING SHELVES, PICTURES 🚗 AND MORE

How to . . . put up shelves

1. **Think about load**. Knowing what weight you're going to put on the shelf will help you decide on the material you use and the number and strength of fixings.

2. **Think about position**. If a shelf is near a door or corridor is it going to get knocked or damaged?

3. **Measure and mark at least twice**. Use a spirit level and a ruler to help you position the shelves correctly – and don't drill any holes until you are sure.

4. **Test for cables**. Use a cable locator and don't fix shelves immediately above or to either side of power sockets.

5. **Use screws and wall plugs that will take the load**. Masonry screws need to go in to a depth of at least 50mm; wood screws to around 40mm, or more if the load is heavy.

6. **Fix it right**. If the shelf is shorter than a metre, fix the brackets to the shelf first, then attach the whole unit to the wall. If the shelf is longer or is heavy, attach the brackets to the wall first, then screw the shelf down on to the brackets.

Pocket tip 🍺

When marking the position of a screw hole in a wall, use a cross, not a dot as this will help you drill straight and avoid 'drift'.

How to . . . hang pictures

1. **Cable check**. As with shelving (see above), you must check for cabling before attaching a picture to the wall.

2. **Fix by weight**. A single brass hook will hold a standard frame up to 1m × 500mm approximately. Anything bigger or heavier than this will need a double strength hook or ideally more than one hook.

3. **Mirrors and heavy pictures**. These should be fixed to the wall with screws and wall plugs for extra strength.

Seven wonders of the ancient world: some old fashioned DIY

- *The Great Pyramid at Giza. The only remaining wonder on the list.*
- *The Hanging Gardens of Babylon. Built in what is now Iraq.*
- *The Colossus of Rhodes. A 100ft statue of the god Helios, which collapsed following an earthquake*
- *Statue of Zeus at Olympia. Another massive statue created by the Greeks and destroyed in a fire after being taken as a trophy by Turk invaders.*

- **The Temple of Artemis at Ephesus**. *Built by the ancient Greeks on a site which is in modern-day Turkey. Only the ruins remain, sadly.*
- **The Mausoleum at Halicarnassus**. *Huge tomb, built for King Mausolus of Persia, who gives his name to this kind of tomb. The stone was robbed by crusaders in the 16th century.*
- **Pharos Lighthouse in Alexandria**. *Nearly 180m in height — its light was visible for distances of up to 35 miles.*

And some modern ones . . .

- *Akashi-Kaikyo Bridge in Japan is nearly 2km in length.*
- *Seikan Tunnel, also in Japan, is 54km long, while the Channel Tunnel between England and France is a close second at 50km.*

How to . . . put up a curtain track or pole

Curtain tracks and poles need to be wider than the window. You'll need about 50–100mm overhang each side.

1. Hold the track up to the window to make sure you've got the right size. As well as being longer, your track/pole needs to be about 50mm higher than the window too.

2. Use a spirit level and straight edge to mark out other wall brackets at regular intervals.

3. Check the wall for cabling and then drill the holes. Now screw the end brackets and any other wall brackets into position with the right size of wall plug.

4. For tracks you'll then need to clip the track into place on the wall brackets.

5. Place the end stops on the track once it is securely fixed to the brackets.

DIY quick fixes

- *A roll of newspaper makes a handy funnel.*
- *Use tights to strain lumps and grit out of paint.*
- *Uncooked spaghetti is a simple replacement for tile spacers.*
- *Spent matchsticks can be used instead of wall plugs.*
- *A bulldog clip makes an effective emergency scraper.*

🚗 ELECTRICAL MAINTENANCE 🚗

How to . . . wire a plug

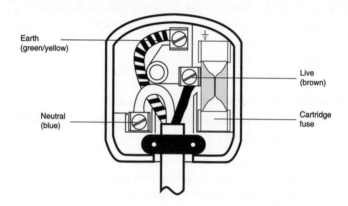

Earth (green/yellow)

Live (brown)

Neutral (blue)

Cartridge fuse

Electrical appliances come with a moulded plug, but if you damage a plug or need to remove one, you'll also need to know how to rewire one. When wiring a plug remember red or brown wire is live, blue or black is neutral and green/yellow or bare is earth.

1. First unscrew the plug. Strip the insulation from the flex to expose the core wires. Lay the wires over the open plug and trim to the right length.

2. Then strip the insulation from the individual wires, loosen the screws of the pillar terminal and insert the wires into the correct terminal.

3. Finally re-tighten the screws to clamp the wires in the terminals and make sure the wires are tight and secure. Then clamp the flex into the cord grip at the entrance to the plug.

How to . . . change light bulbs and fuses

Fuses

There are three main types of fuse box: removable wire fuses, which are old-fashioned and potentially dangerous; cartridge fuses, which are a more modern version of the wire fuse but can be fiddly to test – you'll need a specific electrician's tool called a continuity tester; and MCB (miniature circuit breakers), by far the most common type of fuse and standard in all new houses and new electrical installations. They are trip switches which break the circuit in the event of a problem. They don't need to be replaced, simply reset.

Whatever type of fuse you've got, the problem of a blown fuse is likely to come down to the same issues – an overloaded circuit or a faulty appliance. Switch off the mains power, replace any blown fuses and remove all the appliances. Then reinstall them one by one until the fuse blows again. Once you've identified your faulty appliance, get it repaired professionally.

Bulbs

Another reason for power failure is a blown bulb tripping the MCB or blowing the circuit fuse. Check all the bulbs in the house – if they're traditional filament types, you'll be able to tell if one has blown by giving it a gentle shake – the filament wire will rattle. Replace the bulb and reset the system. If the light is part of a lamp plugged in to the main circuit via a socket, check the fuse in the plug as well as the bulb. Always use a soft, dry cloth or tea towel to remove a bulb that's just blown as it'll be hot.

🚗 WATER MAINTENANCE 🚗

How to . . . bleed a radiator

Bleeding radiators regularly helps to remove air bubbles from the system. This makes them run more smoothly and effectively.

1. You'll need to get hold of a bleed key: a small brass apparatus available from most DIY stores.

2. Make sure the central heating system is off first. Then place the bleed key into the valve at the top of the radiator and turn gently.

3. Wait for all the excess air to be released before tightening the key again. You will see water when it is all gone.

4. Don't forget to hold a piece of rag or kitchen towel beneath the bleed key as you turn the radiator valve. Water in your central heating system is black and will seriously stain floors and paintwork.

How to . . . mend a dripping tap

1. Replace the washer. A leak at the bottom of the tap's handle section shows the washer has failed. Turn off the water supply, empty the pipe of water and remove the head of the tap, replace the washer, use a little oil or WD40 to lubricate and then reattach.

2. Replace or tighten O-ring or packing gland. These can be found around the spindle of the tap (an O-ring is the more modern variant) and can be shown by a leak from the top of the tap handle. You may not need to replace the ring, just tighten the gland nut on top of the headgear (the main part of the handle mechanism). If this doesn't fix the leak, take the tap apart and replace the ring.

How to . . . unblock pipes

Sink wastes

These can be cleared with household drain cleaner – though only if there's no standing water. Otherwise, bale out the excess water and use washing soda and boiling water. If the blockage is caused by solidified fat, heat the waste trap with a hairdryer. For tougher blockages, use a plunger or remove the waste pipe trap altogether to clear it out properly. Remember, if you have to take the waste pipe trap off, it will be full of water (don't be tempted to empty it down the sink!) so keep a bucket handy.

Toilet blockages

These occur when someone's put something unsuitable down the pan. The best, non-chemical options are plunging and rodding with a 'plumber's snake' – a metal spiral that works like mini drain rods.

Exterior drain blockages

The best tool for this job is a decent set of drain rods. You can hire them cheaply, or get your own if you have troublesome drains. Remove the drain cover, feed the rods slowly into the drain, firmly adding sections one at a time and trying not to twist the rods too much. Push with a 'plunger' attachment until you dislodge the blockage, or pull the obstruction back with the corkscrew.

🚗 DECORATING 🚗

How to . . . put up wallpaper

If you've never hung wallpaper before you can get into a real mess if you don't think ahead. Here are some key principles:

1. **Choose the right paper**. Get the heaviest, strongest paper you can. Vinyl paper is the toughest – it will cope with your first fumbling efforts much better than a cheap, thin paper. First-time wallpaper hangers should avoid patterned paper.

2. **Choose the right paste**. Use an all-purpose ready mixed paste. This may be a bit more expensive than other types of paste, but it will give you a good finish first time.

3. **Get enough paper**. Measure the room as if it is a box – don't allow for doors or windows as you will need extra paper to go round odd shapes. Buy at least one more roll than you need.

4. **Prepare carefully**. Make sure the walls are clean and free of dust, and that the surface you're going to paper is in good condition. Never paper over old wallpaper; always remove it

first, using a steamer paper stripper or by soaking the wallpaper with warm water. If you're going over plaster that is very dry, apply plenty of 'size' (half-diluted wallpaper paste) on it first.

5. **Hang it right**. Start from a good vertical line drawn on the wall just in from one corner of the room. Make the line using a plumb line, spirit level and pencil. Soak the first sheet of paper in paste then leave for up to five minutes before hanging it. Paste up a new sheet of paper before hanging the previous one, so that you don't have any unnecessary waiting around. Then hang the first sheet, making sure you align it with your perfect vertical line. Align subsequent sheets to each piece of perfectly plumbed paper and the paper will look ok.

Pocket tip 🍺

When you've finished wallpapering a room, make a note of the number of rolls you used on top of the door frame. The next time you come to paper the room, you'll know exactly what to buy. Simple.

Top ten injury-prone DIY projects

1. Woodworking
2. Laying paving or concrete
3. Hammering nails
4. Cutting and moving bars and sheets of metal
5. Laying bricks
6. Painting
7. Pasting and glueing
8. Screwing in screws
9. Flooring and wall tiling
10. Wallpapering

GENERAL KNOW-HOW

*When I was a boy of 14 my father was so ignorant I could hardly stand
to have the old man around. But when I got to be 21, I was astonished
at how much the old man had learned in seven years.*
Attributed to Mark Twain

🚗 SEWING 🚗

How to . . . sew on a button

Sewing is a dying art, mainly because clothes are now so cheap
and readily available that they are almost literally disposable. The
only practical area of this skill that you must master is sewing on
a button:

1. Find a matching replacement button, some suitable thread
   (about 50cm of thread will do the job) and a needle.

2. Lick the end of the thread and feed it through the eye of the
   needle. Tie the two loose ends of the thread together so
   you've got a loop.

3. Starting from the inside of the shirt, push the needle through
   the fabric then through the hole in the button. Feed back
   through the next buttonhole and back through the fabric.
   Repeat this a couple more times until the button is securely
   fastened – but be sure to leave a little bit of slack between
   the button and the fabric. Make your last couple of pushes of
   the needle through the fabric only, so that you have a knot of
   thread on the inside of the shirt, which you can tie-off to
   hold the button in place.

4. Cut off any remaining thread with scissors.

How to . . . tie knots

There are three simple knots that everyone should be able to master: the reef knot, the sheet bend and the clove hitch. The first two are knots for attaching two pieces of rope together, the third is for attaching rope to another object.

Reef knot. Take the two pieces of rope and wrap the ends right over left. Then repeat the action but this time wrap the left piece over the right and tighten.

Sheet bend. Loop one piece of rope and pass the other piece through the loop, around the outside of the looped rope

and then passing back through the loop once again before tightening.

Clove hitch. Wrap a piece of rope around a post or pole, cross the loose end downwards over the wrapped rope and then feed it

back up underneath the wrapped rope and tighten. This is a good knot to use for climbing or for temporarily securing something as it can be easily undone.

Pocket fact 🔔

Laughing makes you healthier by reducing stress and boosting your immune system. The average child laughs up to 300 times a day. The average adult laughs around 15 times. Go figure.

🚗 FIRST AID 🚗

PERFORMING BASIC FIRST AID

A basic knowledge of first aid is a potential life-saver in an emergency situation. The more you know, the more likely you are to find the right response at the right time, but there's no substitute for hand-on practice. Enrol on a St John Ambulance first aid course – these are run throughout the country and are very cheap and very worthwhile ways to spend a day learning key skills.

In the meantime, you need to know enough to get you through most common emergencies.

If you find yourself in any emergency situation shout for help and call an ambulance as soon as possible.

Assess the casualty. If you're dealing with a person who has collapsed, try to get them to answer a basic question. If they can answer, deal with the situation as explained below. If they give no response and don't respond to a gentle shake of the shoulders (incredibly gentle in the case of a young child), you will need to roll them onto their back and check further to make sure the casualty is breathing. Lift their chin and tilt their head back to open the airway and stop their tongue from lolling back in their throat.

Mouth-to-mouth. If the casualty isn't breathing, you'll need to give mouth-to-mouth ventilation. Clear the mouth of any obvious blockages, pinch the nose and put your lips around the casualty's lips, blowing into their mouth until their chest rises. Repeat this once more and then check the pulse. With a child or baby you should give five breaths. As soon as there are signs of recovery make sure an ambulance is called. If there are no signs of recovery call an ambulance and carry on with mouth-to-mouth and CPR.

Pocket fact 🔔

It is physically impossible to kill yourself by holding your breath.

CPR. If you can't get any signs of recovery from mouth-to-mouth after a couple of attempts, move to CPR. Find the point on the lower chest where the breastbone meets the ribs with one hand, place your other hand on top with fingers interlocked, then, leaning over the casualty, press down on the breastbone, pushing it down by up to 5cm. Do around 15 pushes at a rate of about 100 per minute. Give a couple of breaths of mouth-to-mouth and then repeat. For a baby use just two fingers of one hand to press down and press five times; for a child use the heel of one hand only for five depressions. Continue with mouth-to-mouth breaths between CPR sessions.

Choking. If the casualty is choking, bend them forwards and give them a strong slap between the shoulder blades. If this doesn't work, hold them from behind, linking your hands in fists below the ribs, then pull in and up. Repeat this up to five times. For babies, start by slapping the back then use the chest thrusts outlined above to try to clear any blockage.

Bleeding. Cover the wound with a sterile dressing but don't use a tourniquet. Put pressure on the wound with your fingers instead. Lie the casualty on the floor and raise the injury above head height if possible.

Burns. The main aim is to cool the burn as quickly as you can. Pour cold water on to the burn for up to 10 minutes, then cover it and seek treatment.

Pocket fact 🏌

There are 206 bones in the adult human body, a quarter of which are in the feet.

🚗 ETIQUETTE 🚗

GRACE AND TOASTS

Speaking at a formal occasion is basically a matter of good preparation and clarity of purpose – whether you're saying grace, giving a toast or simply thanking everyone for coming.

Grace. The most simple, commonly recognised form of 'grace' is a short prayer – 'For what we are about to receive, may the Lord make us truly thankful', which should be followed by a quiet 'Amen' from the guests. You can use your own secular equivalents if you're not in a religious environment, such as: 'For what we are about to receive, we are truly thankful'. Do try to keep it short and fairly formal in tone.

A toast (or a reply). Other than a speech (which we'll come to later), this is likely to be the only circumstance in which you'll be asked to stand before a crowd of people and speak formally. Some of the rules of public speaking apply here – for example, you should keep your words to a minimum; don't waffle on about some obscure anecdote. If you're toasting a guest, ask everyone except the recipient of the toast to stand and then explain why you are giving the honour. Don't be crude, don't resort to hyperbole (ie he's the most wonderful friend a man could ever have) as it can be embarrassing, and don't make everyone stand up for ages. If you're nervous about the content, look in a dictionary of quotations for something that you can apply to the recipient. If you are giving a reply, keep it short, polite and in the same spirit and tone as the toast.

Rank/Title	Spoken address	Letter	Envelope
DOCTOR	Doctor	Dear Doctor	Doctor X
ARCHBISHOP (CofE)	Your Grace	Your Excellency	The Most Reverend x. Archbishop of y.
QUEEN	Your Majesty (on introduction), then Ma'am, pronounced: 'Mum'	Madam, with my humble duty	Her Majesty the Queen
PRESIDENT	Mr President	Mr President	The President
JUDGE (HIGH COURT)	My Lord/Lady, Your Lordship/Ladyship	My Lord/Lady	The Hon. Mr/Mrs Justice x.

How to . . . write a wedding speech

At a traditional wedding the toasts (and speeches) have a fixed structure. First up is the father of the bride, who proposes a toast to the bride and groom. Then the groom thanks his new father-in-law, makes his speech and proposes a toast to the bridesmaids. Finally the best man answers on behalf of the bridesmaids, makes his speech and proposes a toast to the parents of the bride and groom. Sometimes, if the father of the bride hasn't opened proceedings, he then stands and says a few words of thanks to the guests.

Whatever your role in a wedding, the rules of making a speech are the same. Follow these basic steps for success:

1. **Don't overdo it**. Your speech should be a couple of minutes in length. It doesn't need to be funny, but there's no harm in putting in a couple of touching anecdotes. A famous or humorous quote will help you to get started. You might also think about quoting some poetry with particular significance.

2. **Be honest**. Say what your daughter/friend/wife means to you, but don't go overboard. A touching childhood story means more than false praise. Don't forget to mention how much you like their choice of partner too.

3. **Don't try to be rude or crude**. Weddings are family occasions and will be full of kids, grannies and easily offended relations.

4. **Make notes.**Write the speech out in full, then extract notes on index cards to help you remember what you wanted to say – keep these notes with you, not the whole speech.

5. **Try it out on a trusted friend**. If they think it is good, you'll be fine.

6. **Relax and remember you're among friends**. This is not a presentation to the board, so just enjoy it and act naturally.

7. **Don't drink too much beforehand**. Actors never drink before a performance, and this is a performance of sorts. The odd glass of champagne is ok, but any more and you're likely to forget your words and cause a lot of embarrassment.

8. **Finish with a flourish**. If you're the father of the bride end with the following phrase: 'Ladies and gentlemen, let's join together in wishing them happiness in their long lives together. I give you the toast of _____ and ___, the bride and groom.'

How to . . . write a formal letter

In the age of electronic communication we are losing the art of the formal letter in all but the most specific business environments (such as the law). But in truth you still can't beat a good stiff formal letter of complaint to get things done properly, or a really effective letter of application to impress a potential new employer. Here's how to do it:

1. **Opening and closing**. Unless you're addressing a specific dignitary (see chart above for official forms of address), you'll open with 'Dear Mr/Mrs/Ms _____', and close with 'Yours sincerely_____'. If you're not addressing the letter by name, you'll use 'Dear Sir or Madam' and 'Yours faithfully_____.'

2. **Structure of the letter**. Whatever the letter is for, it should follow the same basic structure.

- Firstly, start with a statement of purpose: 'I am writing to introduce myself/complain/apply for . . .' and give all the basic information.

- The next paragraph outlines the main points of your letter.

- The third paragraph should ask for action from the person you're writing to and the fourth should explain your next move.

- Finish with 'I look forward to hearing from you soon'.

3. **Tone of the letter**. Use formal language (such as 'require' instead of 'need', 'assist' instead of 'help') and don't use contracted forms (such as 'I've' or 'you're'). Sentences tend to be longer and more complex in a formal letter too, with ideas linked by words that state purpose (therefore) or contrast (although).

4. **A touch of class**. Although it sounds daft, first impressions really do count with a formal letter, so make the effort to use really nice paper and a good quality envelope. Half of the attraction of a letter comes from its feel in the hand, and good stationery does a great job.

Pocket fact

The 10 most common written words in the English language are:

1. the;	6. a;
2. of;	7. for;
3. to;	8. was;
4. in;	9. is;
5. and;	10. that.

🚗 SURVIVAL 🚗

How to . . . survive anything

Survival skills aren't part of every dad's life toolbox, but here are some useful tips for extraordinary situations:

1. **Bear attack**. Bears will lose interest if you lie down and play dead.

2. **Big cat attack**. Unlike bears, big cats (such as mountain lions) love a body to play with, so don't play dead (unless you want to be dead). Instead, open out your coat to make yourself as big as possible, flap it around and make a racket. It may not put them off, but it will make them think twice.

3. **Shark attack**. Attack a shark around the gills or eyes as these are the weakest points.

4. **Submerged car**. If you end up in a river don't try to keep the water out – you need to balance the water pressure so you can get the door open. The best way to do this is to open the windows and let the water in.

🚗 FAMILY AND PETS 🚗

How to . . . get a tick out of a dog

Any dog that romps around in long grass is eventually going to end up with a tick – a nasty blood-sucking parasite that will cause intense scratching and irritation. They are horrid little things that look as if they're made of leather. Their bodies swell as they suck the blood from your pet with half their body buried deep into the poor mutt's skin.

The key is to get this beast out of your dog's skin intact. Ticks are unbelievably tough and trying to remove one with tweezers will cause it to cling even tighter, and will also give your pet some real pain. Even worse, it may lead to you pulling half the tick away and leaving the buried part behind to get infected.

1. You need to relax the tick, and the best way to do that is to get it drunk. Put some strong alcohol (vodka always seems to work best) on a cloth and hold it gently against the tick for a minute or so.

2. Now try to gently extract the tick with the tweezers. There may well still be some resistance, so try a couple of times instead of pulling too hard.

3. Make sure you get the whole tick out and then wash the affected area carefully.

How to . . . photograph your children

1. **Don't get tiny kids to pose**. Most small children are at their most natural when they aren't focused on the camera. Give them something to look at or play with and be prepared to take a lot of bad shots – and one outstanding one.

2. **Involve older children**. Older kids love the immediacy of digital cameras, so tell them what kind of picture you want to take before you take it. They're more likely to play ball so they can see the results on screen straight away.

MOTHER'S DAY

Here's a tricky one. When do you step back and let your children take responsibility, or lack of it, for their contributions on Mother's Day?

- **The early years**. Obviously, while your children are very young, their contributions are minimal and you should make the effort on their behalf – after all you are partly responsible for your partner becoming a mother in the first place. So a meal out or special treat would give her a special day and earn you brownie points.

- **Make and do**. When the children are old enough to be aware of the meaning of Mother's Day you need to coordinate their efforts to show their love for mum – a session of card-making, or a giant banner that you've all helped to decorate will touch her every bit as much as a day in a health spa (well, almost as much).

- **Letting go?** You'll always be grateful to your partner (and to your mother for that matter) for giving birth, so you may want to continue celebrating Mother's Day privately. But eventually you will need to stand back and let the kids make their own contributions in their own way. You can still check behind the scenes that they are doing something, but the more you allow them to make their own choice of gift, the less it will feel like an obligation.

Pocket fact 🏌

Although the idea of honouring fathers goes back many thousands of years, the actual celebration of Father's Day began in 1909. It was started by an American Sonora Dodd who wanted to mark the significant contribution her father had made in bringing up his family. In 1966 the then US president Lyndon Johnson declared the third Sunday in June to be Father's Day and in the USA and UK it has remained as a moveable feast since that day.

Wedding anniversaries and their associated gifts

1st – cotton	**14th** – ivory
2nd – paper	**15th** – crystal
3rd – leather	**20th** – china
4th – flowers	**25th** – silver
5th – wood	**30th** – pearl
6th – iron	**35th** – coral
7th – wool	**40th** – ruby
8th – pottery	**45th** – sapphire
9th – copper	**50th** – gold
10th – tin	**55th** – emerald
11th – steel	**60th** – diamond
12th – silk	**70th** – platinum
13th – lace	

GETTING ON WITH YOUR CHILD'S BOYFRIEND/GIRLFRIEND/PARTNER

It's inevitable that at some stage your child will bring a boyfriend/girlfriend home with them. You will be judged on how you react to this event and so you need to strike a very careful balance. Let's look at all the possibilities:

She brings home a boyfriend

Your little girl is dating. And she is your little girl, no matter whether she's 12 or 21 years old. The boy that she's with will feel under pressure to make a good impression on you, which will be difficult as you doubtless have a good memory of what you were like – and what you wanted out of life – at his age. But try not to judge the situation too harshly. If he's around her age, his emotional maturity will be a little way short of hers and so he might not be quite the strutting gigolo you're picturing. If you've done your job correctly, you'll have given your daughter a healthy self-respect and a basic understanding of the facts of life. She is in control of her body and what she allows others to do with it – that's not your area of jurisdiction.

What you can do is set the boundaries for behaviour in your home. Give them somewhere to go – a private family room rather than a bedroom if possible – and respect their privacy. Don't fire questions at the boy: let him warm to you in his own time. Your daughter will be desperate for you both to get along, and if you are relaxed with him – even if he appears to be a total loser – she'll either get him to reciprocate or she'll drop him and move on.

He brings home a girlfriend

It's tempting to say 'see above', but we don't often behave the same way towards our sons bringing home a new person. Somehow as a man you feel more relaxed about this. But you should still have some boundaries such as those outlined above – remember that somewhere there's a father worrying about the girl your son is with. And don't be tempted to try to impress the girl by showing off. You may well be George Clooney in your own mind, but you're George Formby in hers.

How to . . . be a step-father

A great step-dad knows his limits and his strengths. Follow the following tips for success:

1. **Be prepared to take time**. Remember that you're in a relationship with your partner, not her child. Over time you

will become a dad, but it is a slow and sometimes difficult process.

2. **Be consistent and trustworthy**. The best way to be accepted as a step-father is to be yourself consistently. Always be ready to help out, and if you volunteer to take an active role in your partner's children's lives, make sure you follow through with your commitment.

3. **Talk to your partner**. Make sure you and your partner present a united front. If the children resent your presence in their relationship with their mother, you can address this together.

4. **Acknowledge the past**. If the children still have contact with their natural father, make sure you give this relationship space. He will always have a special place in their lives and if you attempt to undermine him to strengthen your own position you'll suffer in the long run.

How to . . . prepare to be a grandfather

If you think back to your own grandfather, the chances are you're still likely to feel a deep affection or connection to the old fellow, even if your sole contact was the odd Sunday afternoon and a day or two at Christmas.

There are plenty of different ways to approach becoming a grand-father:

1. **Granddaddy day-care**. You can take the active role and offer to get involved with childcare, babysitting and all. This is especially tempting if you missed out first time around and want to show your 'new man' credentials. But make sure you're not stepping on the toes of your son or son-in-law. He needs the time to become a father himself, and doesn't need you to explain what you would have done in your day – especially if he's well aware that you didn't actually do anything.

2. **Old's cool**. Being a subversive granddad is possibly the most dangerous approach – it will either pay off when your

grandkids think you are fantastic for playing hip-hop in the car or doing hilarious impersonations of their dad, or it will fall flat when they cringe with embarrassment when you attempt to run at the school sports day. There's nothing wrong with being surprising or unexpected, but leave the sniggering to the kids' uncles – that's what they are there for. You can still get the respect of the kids by being a mentor, someone who has got the wisdom and experience – and most importantly the time – to share with them.

3. **Being there**. Life as a new grandad isn't so different from life as a new dad. You won't make the same mistakes you made before – you'll probably make new ones. But just being around and ready to help when needed is probably the most important thing you can do.

Pocket fact 🖊

The oldest man to father a child is Indian farmer Nanu Ram Jogi, who fathered his 21st child at the age of 90.

GETTING ON WITH THE IN-LAWS

When you become a parent, the dynamic with your in-laws changes as well. Your previously well-balanced relationship may take on a new competitive edge and unless you're prepared for this, you may find yourself with a conflict on your hands. Here are some tips to help you get through:

Talk it over. Discuss their expectations as grandparents – find out if they expect to have regular visits, if they want their grand-children to stay with them, if they are going to make any prepara-tions for such visits like keeping a room spare for naps etc. You should also find out if they plan to make any financial provisions for the next generation too.

Give them space. It can be very easy to judge the way your extended family behave around your children from the perspective of your own beliefs and intentions. But they will have learned different things and will apply different techniques to childcare. Speak to them about anything that really concerns you, but otherwise rest assured that they have experience and the best interests of their grandchildren at heart.

Work together. Just as parenting is an act of supreme teamwork, the same is true for your in-laws (and your parents). You must all keep a consistency of care with the children so that there's no favouritism and no undermining of authority. Your in-laws should acknowledge that the ultimate decisions lie with you and your partner.

It is a wise father that knows his own child.
William Shakespeare

INDEX

PICK UP YOUR PERFECT
POCKET COMPANION TODAY

Handy tips and fascinating trivia on all your favourite subjects. Be enlightened and entertained with every turn of the page.

£9.99
From all good
bookshops